The Jimmy Buffett Concert Handbook

13-Digit ISBN: 978-1-933662-96-1
10-Digit ISBN: 1-933662-96-4

This book may be ordered by mail from the publisher. Please include $2.00 for postage and handling.

Please support your local bookseller first!

Books published by Cider Mill Press Book Publishers are available at special discounts for bulk purchases in the United States by corporations, institutions, and other organizations. For more information, please contact the publisher.

Cider Mill Press Book Publishers
"Where good books are ready for press"
12 Port Farm Road
Kennebunkport, Maine 04046
Visit us on the Web!
www.cidermillpress.com

Designed by Ponderosa Pine Design, Vicky Vaughn Shea
Typography: ITC American Typewriter, Berthold Akzidenz Groteske, Chaparral Pro, Crud, and Zapf Dingbats
Front and back cover photos and illustrations credits: ©2006 Getty Images, ©iStockphoto.com/Kitch Bain, ©iStockphoto.com/joe Cicak, ©iStockphoto.com/Skip ODonnell, ©iStockphoto.com/Nikolai Okhitin, ©iStockphoto.com/Stephanie Phillips, Courtesy of Elaina "Lainy" Mastromarc
Photo and illustration credits on page 158.

Printed in Singapore

1 2 3 4 5 6 7 8 9 0
First Edition

The Jimmy Buffett

Concert Handbook

By Elizabeth & John Encarnacion

CIDER MILL
PRESS

BOOK
PUBLISHERS

Kennebunkport, Maine

Contents

Welcome to Margaritaville

As legendary singer Jimmy Buffett likes to say, Margaritaville isn't a place, it's a state of mind, "somewhere between the Port of Indecision and Southwest of Disorder." Many fans of Buffett's music and philosophy visit Margaritaville each year by attending his concerts, pre-partying in the parking lot, visiting his restaurants, or just raising a glass to this musical master.

If you head to a Jimmy Buffett concert and tailgate, you leave the harsh real world and are immediately introduced and welcomed to a place without strict schedules, a more relaxed way of life. This traveling show is a big beach party, taking advantage of the hot, sunny weather to transport you to the tropics without that scary flight on a tiny puddle jumper. And best of all, you're surrounded by all your friends, carefree music, and tasty concoctions.

Jimmy Buffett's music is about a lifestyle that most of us can only dream of living. That dream is shared by many folks, from all walks of life. In some ways, the people at the shows are a big cross-section of society. You'll find folks who are young and old; sons, daughters, mothers, and fathers; students and retirees; doctors, lawyers, mortgage bankers, secretaries, professional athletes, and so forth. Most of us have obligations or routines in our lives that we view as burdensome, boring, or repetitive. A Jimmy Buffett show offers all of us a chance to escape into another world. The world of Parrotheads.

CHAPTER 1

Who Is Jimmy Buffett?

A Brief History of Jimmy Buffett

You may know Jimmy Buffett as a singer and song-writer, but he's also a best-selling author, a film producer and movie actor, and a successful businessman and restaurateur. In a world of hyphenates, Jimmy's ahead of the pack.

But this plethora of jobs doesn't define Jimmy Buffett. At heart, he's really just someone who has been living his dream for over thirty years. Along the way, he became an entertainer who essentially developed his own genre of music: tropical folk-rock, or Gulf and Western. As he likes to put it, he's had the best summer job ever for the past thirty plus years. That attitude and the escapist lifestyle he represents are inspiration to millions of his devoted fans—the Parrotheads.

Growing up in humble beginnings in Missis-sippi and Alabama, it would have been hard for Jimmy Buffett to imagine how his life would turn out. Then again, you can't really plan a musical and life journey that has no specific map and has continued to evolve to the present day.

Jimmy was raised in the Gulf Coast, where he was first influenced by country, folk, and Cajun music. His grandfather, James Buffett, Sr., was a ship captain and passed down many stories of adventures out on the sea to his grandson. As he grew older, Jimmy originally attended Auburn University in Alabama before eventually graduating with a history degree from the University of Southern Mississippi. While at the latter school, one of his roommates taught him to play the guitar, and he soon decided that being a musician was his calling in life.

After graduation from college, Jimmy moved to Nashville to begin his musical career. Before he signed to a recording deal, he worked as a writer for *Billboard Magazine* in Nashville, Tennessee. After he signed a two-record deal with Barnaby Records, he released his first album, *Down to Earth*, in 1970. Unfortunately, this album's country music sound failed to appeal to the masses and did not sell many copies. The material Jimmy recorded for the second album was mysteriously "lost" by Barnaby Records, only to be "found" and released many years later, after he had found success.

Without immediate prospects in Nashville, Jimmy headed to Miami for a gig, but when he arrived, he realized it wasn't available. Add in the fact that he was now broke, and Jimmy's life wasn't going so well. Fortunately, Jimmy's friend Jerry Jeff Walker gave him a place to stay for a few months.

From Miami, Jimmy and Jerry took a fateful weekend drive to Key West, which would prove to be one of, if not *the* primary influence in Buffett's music. Arriving to find eighty-five degree weather in November, with a sailboat race going on and plenty of bars around, Jimmy discovered a new lifestyle. He quickly decided to stay awhile, and moved to Key West. The rest, as they say, is history.

Jimmy then signed a new deal with ABC-Dunhill Records and released his first post–Key West album, *A White Sport Coat and a Pink Crustacean*, in 1973. This album featured some of what became

Jimmy's more classic songs, including "Why Don't We Get Drunk," "Grapefruit-Juicy Fruit," and "He Went to Paris," and established his unique sound. His next album, *Living and Dying in ¾ Time*, released in 1974, featured the classic ballad "Come Monday," which was his first song to chart.

In 1977, Jimmy released *Changes in Latitudes, Changes in Attitudes*, which included the definitive Buffett song, "Margaritaville." While the album and subsequent follow-ups would only yield modest commercial success, more and more fans began Phlocking to his summer concerts, wearing Hawaiian shirts and parrot hats, leading one of Jimmy's band members to name them Parrotheads, a slightly more colorful version of the Grateful Dead's devoted Deadheads. Soon the concerts evolved into entire spectacles on their own.

In addition to becoming one of the most successful touring performers, Jimmy also began to develop projects in other areas, writing a collection of short stories and several children's picture books, starting the first of many Margaritaville Cafes, and creating his own record label. Over the years, he has continued his successful writing career while also expanding into new business avenues.

In the midst of all of this activity, Jimmy has continued recording and touring, recently returning to his country music roots. His 2003 duet with Alan Jackson on "It's Five O'Clock Somewhere" yielded a number one single on the country music chart. And Jimmy's 2004 album, *License to Chill*, had a Nashville flavor, including several duets with country music artists such as Clint Black and Martina McBride. But the core of Jimmy's business is still the annual tours, which continue to the present day. Still a top concert draw, Jimmy Buffett and the Coral Reefer Band have played to all sold-out shows in recent years.

The Coral Reefer Band

When you go to a Jimmy Buffett show, you're not just watching a guy playing guitar and singing alone on stage. Instead, you're seeing Jimmy Buffett and the Coral Reefer Band, the ever-changing group of musicians he brings along on tour and into the recording studio. The original Coral Reefer Band was a joke, just four imaginary musicians with funny names that Jimmy dreamed up one day—Marvin Gardens, Kay Pasa, Al Vacado, and Kitty Litter. Even the name is a triple entendre, referencing the coral reefs that populate the tropical seas of which Jimmy often sings, a sailing term befitting a Son of a Son of a Sailor, and a slang term for marijuana, the recreational drug that seems to fit with Jimmy's devil-may-care attitude.

Despite this silliness, by 1975 Jimmy was going on tour and needed to form a real Coral Reefer Band. The founding members of this group were Roger Bartlett (lead guitar and backing vocals), Greg Taylor (keyboards and harmonica), Harry Dailey (bass), and Phillip Fajardo (drums).

Over the years, the lineup of the Coral Reefer Band has changed, but it has always been populated by talented musicians who appreciate the Parrothead spirit and laid-back lifestyle. These are just a few of the most prominent members of the band, past and present.

Greg Taylor (Harmonica)

Greg "Fingers" Taylor was a founding member of the Coral Reefer Band and is known as one of the world's best harmonica players (though he acquired his nickname in high school while playing keyboards). He met Jimmy Buffett when they were both attending the University of Southern Mississippi and worked with him on his early albums before signing on to tour with the Coral Reefer Band in 1975. He resigned from the band in 2000, but returned to record on Jimmy's two 2006 albums, the *Hoot* movie soundtrack and *Take the Weather with You*. He has also appeared on stage with Jimmy as a special guest several times since then.

Michael Utley (Keyboards)

Michael Utley has been playing with Jimmy Buffett since 1973, when he recorded on Buffett's third album, *A White Sport Coat and a Pink Crustacean*. He started touring with Jimmy four years later, and has been touring with the band longer than any other active member. Michael has produced eleven of Jimmy's albums and is even mentioned midway through the song "Volcano," when Jimmy says, "Mr. Utley!" just before the keyboard solo.

Doyle Grisham (Steel Pedal Guitar)

A native of Texas who later moved to Nashville to study the steel pedal guitar, Doyle Grisham recorded on several of Jimmy's early albums in the 1970s, starting with *A White Sport Coat and a Pink Crustacean*. However, it wasn't until 1999's *Beach House on the Moon* that Jimmy suggested he tour with the Coral Reefer Band, which he has done every year since.

Mac McAnally (Guitar, Vocals)

A successful singer and songwriter in his own right, Mac McAnally has recorded ten solo studio albums and written several #1 records for other country artists. Mac first recorded with Jimmy on *Coconut Telegraph* in 1981, for which he wrote the song "It's My Job." Since then, he has continued to work with Jimmy, cowriting songs such as "Love in the Library," "Coast of Carolina," and the recent hit, "License to Chill," and touring with the Coral Reefer Band since 1994. In October 2007, Mac was inducted into the Nashville Songwriters Hall of Fame for his contributions to country music.

Robert Greenidge (Steel Drums)

A native of Trinidad, Robert Greenidge started playing steel drums when he was a kid. Since then, he has recorded with two of the Beatles (John Lennon and Ringo Starr), one of the Beach Boys (Brian Wilson), and many other greats. He first recorded with Jimmy in 1983 on *One Particular Harbour* and has been a member of the Coral Reefer Band ever since.

Ralph MacDonald (Percussion)

Before meeting up with Jimmy Buffett, Ralph MacDonald had already served as the percussionist for Harry Belafonte, for whom he cowrote an album entitled *Calypso Carnival*. He also won a Grammy for writing Roberta Flack's hit song, "Where Is the Love." He first appeared with Jimmy on the 1986 album *Floridays* and started touring with the band nine years later.

Peter Mayer (Guitar, Vocals) and Jim Mayer (Bass)

Brothers who grew up in southern India, where their parents were serving as missionaries, Peter and Jim Mayer were in a band called PM with Roger Guth when they played on Jimmy Buffett's 1989 album, *Off to See the Lizard*. They were immediately accepted as part of the Coral Reefer Band, and have been touring with Jimmy since.

Roger Guth (Drums)

Roger Guth joined the Coral Reefer Band with Peter and Jim Mayer in 1989, after playing drums on *Off to See the Lizard*. When he's not touring with Jimmy, Roger returns to his roots, performing with Peter and Jim as a member of The Peter Mayer Group.

John Lovell (Trumpet)

John Lovell got his lucky break when a friend told him Jimmy Buffett was looking for a trumpet player while he was working at a Circuit City store. He recorded on the 1994 release, *Fruitcakes*, and has been touring with the band since 1992.

Tina Gullickson (Vocals)

A vegetarian and supporter of hemp products, Tina Gullickson joined the Coral Reefer Band in the winter of 1995. She first appeared on the 1996 album *Banana Wind*.

Nadirah Shakoor (Vocals)

A former member of the Grammy-winning hip-hop group Arrested Development, Nadirah Shakoor has been performing with the Coral Reefer Band since 1995 and first recorded with Jimmy on 1996's *Banana Wind*.

Jolly Mon Sing:
The Annotated Buffett Discography

1970 *Down to Earth* (Barnaby Records)

The debut album, known mostly for its lack of success, also features Jimmy's tribute to his grandfather, "The Captain and the Kid."

1971 *High Cumberland Jubilee* (Barnaby Records)

The album that disappeared until Jimmy had achieved success. The title track is probably its best song.

1973 *A White Sport Coat and a Pink Crustacean* (ABC-Dunhill)

The Key West influence is immediately noticeable, with classic songs like "Grapefruit-Juicy Fruit," "Why Don't We Get Drunk," and "He Went to Paris." There are still some country roots evident with "The Great Filling Station Holdup," but even that song has lyrics about drinking.

1974 *Living and Dying in ¾ Time* (ABC-Dunhill)
"Come Monday" is notable as the first Buffett song to climb the music charts.

1974 *A1A* (ABC-Dunhill)
"A Pirate Looks at Forty" and "Tin Cup Chalice" are among Jimmy's best ballads. A1A, of course, is a reference to the Florida state road that runs all the way to Key West.

1975 *Rancho Deluxe* (United Artists)
"Livingston Saturday Night" highlights this film soundtrack. This Western comedy is actually quite entertaining.

1976 *Havana Daydreamin'* (ABC)
"The Captain and the Kid" is rereleased on this album, and the title track brilliantly describes a warm, tropical setting.

1978 *Changes in Latitudes, Changes in Attitudes* (ABC)

"Margaritaville" is the Parrothead anthem, and "Changes in Latitudes, Changes in Attitudes" is now highlighted as the "video" portion of concerts.

1978 *Son of a Son of a Sailor* (ABC)

"Son of a Son of a Sailor" describes Jimmy's quest for adventure, and "Cheeseburger in Paradise" tells of his quest to satisfy his carnivorous appetite.

1978 *You Had to Be There* (MCA)

This two-disc live album was recorded at tour stops in Atlanta and Miami.

1979 *Volcano* (MCA)

"Fins" and "Volcano" have become concert staples.

1981 *Coconut Telegraph* (MCA)

"The Weather Is Here, Wish You Were Beautiful" is probably one of Jimmy's more humorous songs. "Growing Older But Not Up" is also a terrific motto.

1981 *Somewhere Over China* (MCA)

Jimmy sings inaccurately that "It's Midnight and I'm Not Famous Yet."

1983 *One Particular Harbour* (MCA)

The title song vividly describes the perfect destination. Concert classic "Brown Eyed Girl" is also on the album.

1984 *Riddles in the Sand* (MCA)

"Knees of My Heart" highlights the album's tracks.

1985 *Last Mango in Paris* (MCA)

One of Jimmy's recurring themes in his songs is characters relating personal stories, and "Last Mango in Paris" is an excellent example of this type of song. Three singles from the album made the country music charts.

1985 *Songs You Know By Heart* (MCA)

This greatest hits album is perfect for very casual Buffett fans as well as for folks who've just discovered his music and need a "starter" album.

1986 *Floridays* (MCA)

"You'll Never Work in Dis Bidness Again" is tinged with sarcasm for those who try to make it in the entertainment business but are rebuffed. The album as a whole is not one of his best works.

1988 *Hot Water* (MCA)

"Homemade Music" and "Smart Woman (In a Real Short Skirt)" are some of the better songs on this album.

1989 *Off to See the Lizard* (MCA)

"The Pascagoula Run" is Jimmy's tip of his hat to his birthplace.

1990 *Feeding Frenzy* (MCA)

This live album was recorded in Cincinnati and Atlanta. The version of "One Particular Harbour" is excellent.

1992 *Boats, Beaches, Bars, & Ballads* (Margaritaville/MCA)

This four CD box set is perfect for the Parrothead looking to quickly catch up on Buffett's discography without having to purchase all of his other albums.

1993 *Before the Beach* (MCA)

This release is just the rerelease of Jimmy's two pre–Key West albums.

1994 *Fruitcakes* (Margaritaville/MCA)

Jimmy's first studio album in five years features an enjoyable mix of songs. The entire album, including the title track, "Lone Palm," and covers of "Uncle John's Band" and "Sunny Afternoon," is consistently strong.

1995 *Barometer Soup* (Margaritaville/MCA)

Buffett's cover of "Mexico" includes a superb intro, and the title track is also top notch.

1996 *Banana Wind* (Margaritaville/MCA)

The album is a little more mellow than the previous two releases. "Jamaica Mistaica" relates Buffett's harrowing experience in Jamaica. "False Echoes" includes a hidden track about ten minutes into it.

1996 *Christmas Island* (Margaritaville/MCA)

Buffett records his first Christmas album, with a tropical feel, of course.

1998 *Don't Stop the Carnival* **(Margaritaville/Island)**

This musical based on the Herman Wouk book didn't last too long, but the soundtrack isn't bad. "Public Relations" is among the stronger tracks.

1999 *Beach House on the Moon* **(Margaritaville/Island)**

The high energy "I Will Play for Gumbo" has turned into a concert favorite.

1999 *Buffett Live: Tuesdays, Thursdays, Saturdays* **(Mailboat)**

This live album contains songs that were recorded throughout the 1998 and 1999 tours. This recording of "Margaritaville" includes the "lost" verse.

2002 *Far Side of the World* **(Mailboat)**

This album is a slight departure from Jimmy's usual tropical music, and returns to a more folk-based sound. "All the Ways I Want You" is a stirring ballad.

2003 *Meet Me in Margaritaville* **(UTV/MCA/Mailboat)**

More of a two-disc mix of old and newer tracks, such as "School Boy Heart" and "Fruitcakes," than a greatest hits collection. There are several new and live recordings interspersed.

2004 *License to Chill* **(RCA Nashville)**

Buffett delivers an album with significant country music influences. "Hey Good Lookin'," "Trip Around the Sun," and "Scarlet Begonias" provide highlights.

2006 *Take the Weather with You* **(RCA Nashville/Mailboat)**

The most recent album takes shots at cell phone usage in "Everybody's on the Phone," and at the threat of terrorism in "Party at the End of the World."

I Will Play for Gumbo:
The Jimmy Buffett Tourography

Jimmy Buffett's studio albums are great, but to really experience his music one needs to see him live. Unlike most musicians, who only tour to support a new album, Jimmy has been traveling every year to visit his Phlock of Parrotheads since his first tour in 1973. Jimmy likes colorful, creative names, so he christens each new tour with a unique moniker, often derived from an album or song title.

The sets change each year to fit the mood of the theme, adding to the visual interest of the show, but the theme is always beachy and tropical. Fans add to this coastal feeling by wearing Hawaiian shirts and grass skirts, bouncing beach balls up in the air, and dancing barefoot in the aisles.

Always an adventurer, Jimmy likes to add a few new locales to the mix each year, while still visiting many old favorites. He often favors outdoor amphitheater-style venues that suit the casual atmosphere of his concerts.

1973: 1973 Tour, 4 shows
New Cities: San Anselmo, CA

1974: 1974 Tour, 22 shows
New Cities: Key West, FL; Cambridge, MA; Los Angeles, CA; Sausalito, CA; Springfield, IL; Houston, TX; Nashville, TN; Bryn Mawr, PA; College Station, TX; San Francisco, CA

1975: 1975 Tour, 18 shows
New Cities: Florence, AL; New York, NY; Milwaukee, WI; Portland, OR; Austin, TX; San Diego, CA; Washington, DC

1976: A Pink Crustacean Tour, 24 shows
New Cities: Kelowna, BC, Canada; Gainesville, FL; Berkeley, CA; Eugene, OR; Miami, FL; New Orleans, LA; Charlotte, NC; Atlanta, GA; Nashville, TN; Greensboro, NC; Huntsville, AL; Reno, NV; Edmonton, AB, Canada

1977: 1977 Tour, 41 shows

New Cities: Dothan, AL; Savannah, GA; Clemson, SC; Springfield, MA; Uniondale, NY; Rochester, NY; Largo, MD; Richmond, VA; Norfolk, VA; New Haven, CT; Binghamton, NY; Montreal, QE, Canada; Toronto, ON, Canada; Richfield, OH; Santa Monica, CA; San Jose, CA; Orlando, FL; Kansas City, KS; Hoffman Estates, IL; Columbia, MD; Cuyahoga Falls, OH; Pittsburgh, PA; Denver, CO; Jackson, MS; Durham, NC; Winnipeg, AB, Canada; Seattle, WA

1978: Cheeseburger in Paradise Tour, 26 shows

New Cities: Providence, RI; Commack, NY; St. Paul, MN; Lincoln, NE; Sultan, WA; Angels Camp, CA; Biloxi, MS

1979: You Had to Be There/Volcano Tour, 19 shows

New Cities: Tuscaloosa, AL; Dallas, TX, San Antonio, TX; Lubbock, TX; Tempe, AZ; Murfreesboro, TN; Philadelphia, PA; Honolulu, HI; Pullman, WA

1980: Hotdog and Roadmap Tour, 25 shows

New Cities: Columbia, SC; Boston, MA; Minneapolis, MN; Hattiesburg, MS; East Lansing, MI

1981: Coconut Telegraph Tour, 17 shows

New Cities: West Palm Beach, FL; Lakeland, FL; St. Petersburg, FL; Indianapolis, IN; Rochester Hills, MI

1982: Homecoming Tour, 26 shows

New Cities: Lake Tahoe, CA; Boulder, CO; Norman, OK; Waikiki, HI; Papeete, Tahiti; Irvine, CA; Phoenix, AZ; Kansas City, MO; Clarkston, MI; San Bernardino, CA; Devore, CA; Chapel Hill, NC; Cumming, GA; Johnson City, TN; Tampa, FL; Montego Bay, Jamaica

1983: Somewhere Over China Tour, 25 shows

New Cities: Cleveland, OH; Bloomington, IN; Maui, HI; Telluride, CO; Oxford, OH; Augusta, GA

1984: Feeding Frenzy Tour, 15 shows

New Cities: Fremantle, Australia; Cincinnati, OH; Memphis, TN; Sunrise, FL

1985: Sleepless Knights Tour, 40 shows

New Cities: Tucson, AZ; Evansville, IN; Louisville, KY; Holmdel, NJ; Portland, ME; Doswell, VA; Omaha, NE; Oklahoma City, OK; Wantagh, NY; Champaign, IL; Daytona Beach, FL

The Jimmy Buffett Concert Handbook

1986: Floridays Tour/World Tour of Florida, 55 shows

New Cities: St. Louis, MO; Pensacola, FL; Mansfield, MA; Pittsburgh, PA; Sacramento, CA; Concord, CA; Mountain View, CA; Salt Lake City, UT; Arlington, TX; Birmingham, AL; Kona, HI; Palmetto, FL; Auburn, AL; Tallahassee, FL

1987: King Kong Trio Tour/A Pirate Looks at Forty Tour, 54 shows

New Cities: Auckland, New Zealand; Richmond, KY; Fairfax, VA; Harrisburg, VA; Chicago, IL; Bonner Springs, KS; Anchorage, AK

1988: Cheap Vacation Tour/Hot Water Tour, 55 shows

New Cities: Greenville, NC; Worcester, MA; Charlottesville, VA; Boone, NC; East Troy, WI; Costa Mesa, CA; Paso Robles, CA

1989: Off to See the Lizard Tour, 42 shows

New Cities: Auburn Hills, MI; Bristol, CT; Williamsburg, VA; Columbus, OH

1990: Jimmy's Jump Up Tour, 46 shows

New Cities: Grove City, OH; Chattanooga, TN; Winston-Salem, NC; Hilton Head, SC; Burgettstown, PA; Noblesville, IN; Canandaigua, NY; Sarasota Springs, NY

1991: Jump Up Tour/Outpost Tour, 50 shows

New Cities: Baton Rouge, LA; Raleigh, NC; Grove City, OH; Pelham, AL

1992: Recession Recess Tour, 58 shows

New Cities: George, WA; Vancouver, BC, Canada; Lihue, HI; Lahaina, HI

1993: Chameleon Caravan Tour, 51 shows

New Cities: Galveston, TX; Del Mar, CA; Tacoma, WA

1994: Chameleon Caravan Tour/Fruitcakes Tour, 46 shows

New Cities: Mesa, AZ; Knoxville, TN; Ft. Lauderdale, FL; Montauk, NY

1995: Fruitcakes Tour/Domino College Tour, 48 shows
New Cities: Charleston, SC; Columbus, OH; Bristow, VA; Camden, NJ; Hartford, CT

1996: Banana Wind Tour, 48 shows
New Cities: Tinley Park, IL; Virginia Beach, VA; Southampton, NY; Las Vegas, NV

1997: Banana Wind Tour/Havana Daydreamin' Tour, 45 shows
New Cities: Aspen, CO

1998: Havana Daydreamin' Tour/Don't Stop the Carnival Tour, 49 shows
New Cities: Tacoma, WA; Chula Vista, CA

1999: Don't Stop the Carnival Tour/Beach House on the Moon Tour, 38 shows
New Cities: East Hampton, NY

2000: Beach House on the Moon Tour/Tuesdays, Thursdays, Saturdays Tour, 36 shows

2001: Tuesdays, Thursdays, Saturdays Tour/ A Beach Odyssey Tour, 34 shows

New Cities: Oakland, CA; Fairhope, AL

2002: 2002: A Beach Odyssey Tour/Far Side of the World Tour, 36 shows

New Cities: Ocho Rios, Jamaica

2003: Far Side of the World Tour/Tiki Time Tour, 29 shows

New Cities: Auburn, WA; Vancouver, WA

2004: Tiki Time Tour/License to Chill Tour, 34 shows

New Cities: Anaheim, CA

2005: A Salty Piece of Land Tour, 26 shows

New Cities: Jacksonville, FL; Santa Barbara, CA; Uncasville, CT

2006: Party at the End of the World Tour, 29 shows

New Cities: Myrtle Beach, SC

2007: Bama Breeze Tour, 27 shows

New Cities: Anguilla, British Virgin Islands; Frisco, TX; Paris, France; Atlantic City, NJ; Foxboro, MA

Songs You Know By Heart

Jimmy Buffet's songs are so popular because they're escapist, often humorous, and singable. Go to any Jimmy Buffett concert (or really, just about anywhere a Buffett song is playing) and you'll hear everyone singing along. Many of the songs have traditions attached, which make the faithful feel even more connected to the music. Knowing these "insider" audience responses and hand motions is essential to getting the full concert experience.

Learning the stories behind Jimmy's songs is another thing that brings his Phlock together. Parrotheads know that even Jimmy's most outrageous songs often have a kernel of truth to them. Like many singer-songwriters, he mines his personal experiences to come up with ideas for his songs. Over the years, he has shared many of these inspirations with his audience.

Whether you're visiting Margaritaville for the first time or own a time-share there, enjoy this little sampling of Buffett's most revered traditions, legends, and inspirations. These are the songs (and stories) you should know by heart.

The Big 8

Unlike some artists who petulantly refuse to play some of their biggest hits in concert, Jimmy Buffett likes to please his fans by making sure that they almost always get to experience his "Big 8." These eight songs are fan favorites, the songs that even relative newcomers to the Buffett scene can sing along with. For a while, "Why Don't We Get Drunk (And Screw)" was a constant fixture as well, but Jimmy hasn't been playing it much on recent tours. Buffett's most recent hit, "It's Five O'Clock Somewhere," needs a few more years of consistent play before it officially makes this list, but it's fast becoming a strong contender.

1. "Margaritaville"
2. "Cheeseburger in Paradise"
3. "Fins"
4. "Changes in Latitudes, Changes in Attitudes"
5. "Volcano"
6. "A Pirate Looks at Forty"
7. "Come Monday"
8. "One Particular Harbour"

The Jimmy Buffett Concert Handbook

"Margaritaville"

"Margaritaville," of course, is the national anthem of the Parrothead nation, and lends its name to Jimmy Buffett's corporation. The tune is easily Jimmy's most well-known song, probably because it is the embodiment of his ideal lifestyle. A tropical location, beautiful weather, and frozen margaritas—who wouldn't want that?

Jimmy wrote "Margaritaville" while living in Key West, leading some people to mistakenly believe that Margaritaville is based on Key West. Jimmy has frequently stated that Margaritaville isn't a place on a map, but that it's a state of mind. The lyrics reflect a lazy life of drinking margaritas and partying without regard for consequence. During concerts, the Phlock indulges in a bit of audience participation, singing along to the chorus loudly and yelling "Salt, Salt, Salt!" after Jimmy says the word.

Through the years, "Margaritaville" has come to symbolize Jimmy Buffett's career in music as well. His music has not been about receiving critical acclaim, winning awards, and having chart-toppers. Instead, his music is just about enjoying life and chilling out. For legions of Parrotheads, Margaritaville is the ultimate destination.

That Concoction That Helps Me Hang On

Since "Margaritaville" is arguably Jimmy's most famous song, and is the namesake for his business empire and brand, let's spend a few minutes investigating the history of this citrus concoction.

The margarita is probably the most common tequila-based cocktail drink. Margaritas are typically served shaken with ice and strained, on the rocks, or blended with ice. Margarita flavors are plentiful, from the traditional lime, to more exotic flavors like strawberry, mango, and raspberry. There are numerous variations of the drink, but there is one standard formula.

The basic margarita consists of tequila, an orange liqueur such as triple sec or Cointreau, and fresh lime or lemon juice. The ratio of the ingredients can vary, but common ratios include 2:1:1 (2 parts tequila, 1 part triple sec or Cointreau, and 1 part lime or lemon juice), 3:2:1 (3 parts tequila, 2 parts triple sec or Cointreau, 1 part lime or lemon juice), and 1:1:1 (1 part tequila, 1 part triple sec or Cointreau, 1 part lime or lemon juice). A salt-rimmed glass is common, but optional, particularly in these days of high-blood pressure concerns. Alternate liqueurs such as Grand Marnier or Blue Curaçao are sometimes used in place of the triple sec to add to the flavor.

The preparation of the drink is relatively simple. For salted glasses, you rub a lime slice around the outer rim of the glass, then roll the rim in a saucer of kosher salt. The other ingredients are then mixed together with ice in a shaker before being strained into the glass (with ice in it if the drink is served on the rocks). Add the slice of lime to the glass as a garnish, and you now have the standard margarita.

Who Invented the Margarita?

The margarita has probably been around since at least the 1940s, but exactly who created this tasty beverage isn't completely clear. Several folks have laid stake to the claim of inventing the margarita. Here are the main contenders:

1936: Danny Negrete, Garci Crispo hotel in Pueblo, Mexico.

Negrete's family claims that Negrete, who opened the bar with his brother, presented the margarita as a wedding present to his sister-in-law, Margarita.

1938: Carlos "Danny" Herrera, Rancho La Gloria, between Tijuana and Rosarito Beach, Mexico.

The story goes that Herrera was experimenting with a concoction of tequila, Cointreau, and fresh lemon juice. He named it "margarita," likely after a showgirl and actress named Marjorie King, or Rita De La Rosa, who used to stop by the hotel.

1942: Francisco "Pancho" Morales, Tommy's Place, Juárez, Mexico.

Morales reportedly invented the margarita after a woman requested a drink called a Magnolia (brandy, Cointreau, and an egg yolk, topped with Champagne). As he was not sure about the recipe, Morales improvised and made the cocktail we now know as a margarita.

1948: Margaret Sames, Acapulco, Mexico.

Sames may have created the drink at her bar in Acapulco. In fact, Sames may have even added the salt around the glass as a garnish, knowing that people tended to precede drinking tequila by licking salt.

Cheeseburger in Paradise

Walk around the parking lot during a Jimmy Buffett concert, and you're sure to see several people wearing cheeseburgers on their heads. No, they're not handing out McDonald's coupons—they're fans of the classic Buffett song, "Cheeseburger in Paradise."

What exactly *is* a Cheeseburger in Paradise? According to Jimmy's lyrics, it's a delicious cheeseburger, cooked medium-rare in a pre–Mad Cow world and loaded with lettuce, tomato, a slice of onion,

Heinz 57 sauce, and mustard. Jimmy goes on to sing that the burger is accompanied by French fries, a big kosher pickle, and a cold draft beer. But this song isn't really about a specific hamburger. The true message of the lyrics is that after eating the same stuff over and over again (or trying to stay on a healthy diet), a good, basic cheeseburger tastes like a little bite of heaven.

The Legend of the Cheeseburger in Paradise

Over the years, many restaurants have claimed to be the home of the official Cheeseburger in Paradise. They spin stories of how Jimmy Buffett loved their particular burgers so much he wrote the song that cemented their place in history. Buffett himself, however, tells a much different story, of a well-done (and not in the good way) cheeseburger that tasted "like manna from heaven" only because it followed a difficult Caribbean voyage on his first boat, the *Euphoria*.

After a run of bad weather, a broken bowsprit, and a diet of peanut butter and canned foods, Buffett was dreaming of real food—a hot, juicy cheeseburger. When the boat finally landed on the island of Tortola, Buffett and his crew

The Jimmy Buffett Concert Handbook

went straight to the restaurant. Despite its location on an island that was not very well supplied in those days, the restaurant's menu offered American favorites like fancy frozen drinks and, of course, Buffett's dream—cheeseburgers. The burgers and their buns were overcooked, but to those hungry sailors, they tasted like paradise. And so the legend was born.

Fins

Inspired by the sight of a group of men crowding a few beautiful women at a bar, Jimmy Buffett imagined them as sharks circling their bait and wrote a song about it. Now it's a fan favorite, often saved for the last encore and inspiring countless fins on cars in the parking lot.

During the chorus, Parrotheads reach toward the sky with their palms together to form a fin shape (like making a giant *A*). As Jimmy sings about the sharks circling the girl, all the fans rotate their arms in circles above their heads. Then, as he sings, "Fins to the left," everyone leans their "fins" to the left, followed by "Fins to the right." Finally, on the last line of the chorus, the Parrotheads all wave their arms above their heads from side to side. It's like a mini workout during the concert—feel those frozen concoction calories melting away!

Changes in Latitudes, Changes in Attitudes

Though Jimmy doesn't participate in the traditional preconcert tailgate himself, he does send his representatives out to film the bacchanalia. They quickly edit the footage and broadcast it on giant video screens during the concert while Jimmy and the Coral Reefers play "Changes in Latitudes, Changes in Attitudes." Now, you may be wondering, "How can I make it up onto the big screen?"

1. Flash your boobs. The producers love outrageous behavior.
2. Have something in your tailgating setup that's so amazing that they hear about it all over the parking lot. "Did you see the guy who towed a real boat here and decorated it to look like a pirate ship?"
3. Wear a very tacky but clever costume. They're all about things like a pirate walking around with a real parrot on his shoulder and other unusual twists on the typical Parrothead uniform.

4. Create a good-looking T-shirt with a unique, Buffett-inspired image and/or saying. Professional printing is a plus—your fellow fans need to be able to read it on the screen through their drunken haze.

5. Be the epitome of the Buffett tailgate—what they really want to show is people having a heck of a lot of fun.

Why Don't We Get Drunk (And Screw)

This fan favorite was written as a parody of country songs with thinly-veiled sexual references. Jimmy Buffett decided that if country artists were getting away with being so raunchy, he might as well be blunt about the message that they were all sending. Keeping with the spirit of the parody, Jimmy attributed the authorship of "Why Don't We Get Drunk (And Screw)" to imaginary Coral Reefer Band member Marvin Gardens. On April 1, 1989, the *Sarasota Herald-Tribune* even printed an obituary for the dear, departed Marvin as an April Fool's joke. (Or was it?)

These days, Jimmy is sensitive to the large number of fans who bring their children to shows and no longer sings the song at every concert as a matter of course. When he does sing it, he often puts it in a new musical style or plays around with alternate lyrics, such as "Why don't we get milk and moo," or "Why don't we get lunch in school," always ending with the real line.

Son of a Son of a Sailor

Jimmy Buffett figures that about ninety percent of his songs are autobiographical. And so he is indeed the "Son of a Son of a Sailor." Buffett's grandfather, James Buffett, Sr., captained his own five-masted ship across the Atlantic, Pacific, and Caribbean. The senior Buffett passed down to his grandson countless stories of his own adventures and experiences on the ocean. (Another Buffett song, "The Captain and the Kid," relates how Jimmy used to climb up

on his grandfather's knee and listen to the tales of life on the sea). These tales helped inspire Jimmy to go the Caribbean and find out about this way of life for himself. And not surprisingly, these stories from Jimmy's grandfather are easily apparent in the younger Buffett's music.

In essence, "Son of a Son of a Sailor" tells the story of Jimmy's chosen lifestyle. The song relates how he "went out on the sea for adventure" and provides a description of that experience that would make anyone envious. The seafaring life of traveling across the Caribbean, taking the best qualities of "heroes and crooks," drinking rum, and, notably, staying out of any legal entanglements, certainly appeals to many. Perhaps most telling is the last verse of the song, where Buffett sings about how long the lifestyle will continue. The answer is something he can't and doesn't want to pinpoint. Until it ends, he'll continue to cruise along and not resort to the ordinary lives that many others have. And this answer also applies to the annual concert tours, which continue with no immediate end in sight.

Jamaica Mistaica

Some folks try to forget harrowing incidents as quickly as possible. Jimmy Buffett, however, memorialized one in a song.

In 1996, Jimmy Buffett's seaplane, the Hemisphere Dancer, was traveling on the water near Negril when it faced gunfire from Jamaican authorities who mistook it for a drug-runner's plane. Local authorities believed that contraband such as drugs were smuggled in and out of caves near Negril, and that the seaplane was either coming from or going to those caves. Jimmy, of course, had "only come for [Jamaican jerk] chicken" and was not "the ganja plane." Eventually, the misunderstanding was cleared up with no injuries other than some bullet holes in the Hemisphere Dancer.

Likely because of Buffett's long time involvement with the country (including Margaritaville restaurants in Montego Bay, Ocho Rios, and Negril), Jamaican authorities profusely and publicly apologized for the incident. To poke a little fun at it, Buffett penned "Jamaica Mistaica." As far as we know, Jamaican authorities have so far kept the promise not to shoot the Hemisphere Dancer out of the sky again.

It's Five O'Clock Somewhere

This award-winning and chart-topping song features Jimmy Buffett as a guest artist, singing along with Alan Jackson. The entire song epitomizes Buffett's philosophy of finding a way to de-stress in today's hectic world. In fact, when Alan Jackson was originally pitched the song, he immediately thought it sounded like a Buffett tune.

The lyrics tell a simple story of a person who, stressed out at work, decides to head to the bar early, rationalizing that it's not too early to start drinking because "It's five o'clock somewhere." Immediately embraced by the Parrothead faithful despite not appearing on one of Jimmy's studio albums, the song has already become a staple at Buffett concerts, with Mac McAnally singing Alan Jackson's part. It has also quickly become one of the most popular slogans found on signs and T-shirts in the pre-party parking lots.

Semi-True Story:
The Buffett Bookography

Jimmy Buffett has always told stories through his songs, so it's only natural that he'd start writing books. His books have sold well over two million copies, and he joins such literary giants as John Steinbeck and Ernest Hemingway as only the sixth author ever to have had #1 *New York Times* best sellers in both the fiction and nonfiction categories. Not bad for a barefoot singer from the South.

Children's Picture Books

The Jolly Mon **(Harcourt, 1988)**

This pleasant picture book, written with his eldest daughter, Savannah Jane, was based on his song, "Jolly Mon Sing" and comes with a compact disc.

Trouble Dolls **(Harcourt, 1991)**

Another picture book with Savannah Jane, *Trouble Dolls* tells of a young girl trying to find her father, who has been lost in the Everglades.

Adult Nonfiction

A Pirate Looks at Fifty **(Random House, 1998)**

Jimmy's autobiography doubles as a travelogue of a three-week trip through Central and South America in his seaplane, and hit #1 on the *New York Times* best seller list.

Adult Fiction

Tales from Margaritaville **(Harcourt, 1989)**
Jimmy's first book for adults is a satisfying mixture of fictional short stories and autobiographical essays.

Where Is Joe Merchant? **(Harcourt, 1992)**
A rock star disappears, and an unlucky seaplane pilot is recruited to help look for him in Jimmy's first full-length novel for adults—his other #1 best seller.

A Salty Piece of Land **(Little, Brown, 2004)**
This tale of a former cowboy now making a living through fishing in the Caribbean also lent its name to one of Jimmy's concert tours.

Swine Not? **(Little, Brown, 2008)**
A charming story of a potbelly pig living in a Manhattan high-rise, Jimmy's latest novel will appeal to all ages.

You'll Never Work in Dis Bidness Again: The Buffett Brand

In 1985, Jimmy Buffett opened the first Margaritaville Cafe in Key West, Florida. By the end of 2008, no fewer than fifteen additional Margaritaville restaurants and stores will have opened in the southern United States, the Caribbean, and Mexico. Not mere carbon copies of each other, Margaritaville restaurants capture the craziness and excess that are a hallmark of the pre-party tailgates with margarita-erupting volcanoes, a pool slide in the bar, and other flights of fantasy. Each location has its own Web site and online store, reflecting their unique qualities. Jimmy is even teaming with Harrah's Entertainment to build a Margaritaville Casino and Resort in Biloxi, the largest single investment in the area since Hurricane Katrina.

Expanding on the Margaritaville Brand, Jimmy has developed the following products, some of which are available in retail stores and others which are Margaritaville exclusives.

Margaritaville Tequila comes in both gold and silver forms, as well as in five flavored tequilas that are mixed with fruity liqueurs. It has its own Web site at www.margaritavilletequila.com.

- Margaritaville Gold
- Margaritaville Silver
- Calypso Coconut
- Island Lime
- Tropical Tangerine
- Last Mango
- Paradise Passion Fruit

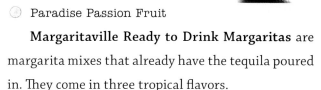

Margaritaville Ready to Drink Margaritas are margarita mixes that already have the tequila poured in. They come in three tropical flavors.

- Classic Lime
- Last Mango
- Passion Fruit

Land Shark Lager is an island lager with a noticeable hop taste. It's currently available at select Margaritaville locations, at some Florida retailers, and at most Buffett tour stops. Full retail listings are available on www.landsharklager.com.

Margaritaville Seafood, which can be found on the Web at www.margaritavilleshrimp.com, includes a line of four flavors of frozen shrimp as well as frozen crab cakes and calamari, all of which are sold in grocery stores nationwide.

- Calypso Coconut Shrimp

- Island Lime Shrimp
- Jammin' Jerk Shrimp
- Sunset Shrimp Scampi
- Coral Reef Crab Cakes
- Captain's Calamari Strips

Margaritaville Chicken is a line of prepackaged chicken wings that come in five flavors and are sold through warehouse clubs such as Sam's Club, Costco, and BJ's.

- Buffalo Chicken Wings
- Honey BBQ Chicken Wings
- Teriyaki Chicken Wings
- Orange Peel Chicken Wings
- Mango Tequila Chicken Wings

The **Margaritaville Frozen Concoction Maker** is a small appliance that blends ice shavings with other ingredients to make margaritas and other Frozen Concoctions. The **Margaritaville Party Cooler** chills frozen drinks from the Concoction Maker as well as bottles and cans. They can both be found on www.margaritavillecargo.com.

Margaritaville Soles of the Tropics is a new line of sandals and casual footwear (perfect for wearing to Buffett shows) that is now available online at www.margaritavilleretail.com/footwear.

Radio Margaritaville is a radio station on Sirius Satellite Radio (also available via streaming audio on the Web) that simulcasts live Jimmy Buffett concerts, replays of older tour stops, tunes from Buffett's extensive library, and songs from other featured artists who pair well with Jimmy's music.

Cheeseburger in Paradise Restaurants

It was only natural that Jimmy Buffett's song about "heaven on earth with an onion slice" would spawn a chain of casual restaurants. Unlike the Margaritaville Cafes, which Jimmy's holding company owns outright, these restaurants were developed in 2002 with Outback Steakhouse's parent company, OSI Restaurant Partners. The Cheeseburger in Paradise restaurants are franchised by OSI under a licensing agreement with Buffett. As of this writing, forty-four Cheeseburger in Paradise locations had opened, mainly centered along the East Coast and near the Great Lakes.

CHAPTER 2

Becoming a Parrothead

We Are the People Our Parents Warned Us About: A Field Guide to the Phlock

At a Buffett show, everyone's welcome because we're all there for the same reason—to have fun. We're all a part of the Phlock—a perfect name for the Parrothead nation. You'll see elderly couples decked out in full tropical attire, chatting with twenty-somethings concentrating on drinking themselves into oblivion. Kids offering free Jello shots to neighboring tailgates, and die-hard Parrotheads piling out of a charter bus. A Buffett pre-party is a virtual utopia of relaxation, entertainment, and frosty beverages. Wondering where you fit in amongst the chaos in the parking lot? Take a look.

The Seasoned Vet

By far, the vast majority of the Buffett tailgate scene is made up of the Seasoned Vets: those among us who have been to multiple shows. As experienced Buffett concertgoers, Seasoned Vets know the routine and are no longer overwhelmed by the scene. While this group includes a wide variety of folks and concert experience (from those fans who have been to three shows to those who have been to thirteen), they share some common traits. Seasoned Vets show up several hours before the concert in the afternoon to party in their own or their friends' tailgates before heading off to the

concert. They know to dress up in Hawaiian shirts or other Buffett-themed apparel. Perhaps just as important, Seasoned Vets know to keep hydrated by mixing in water and soda with alcoholic beverages. During the actual concert, Seasoned Vets are also more than familiar with all the songs and their routines.

The Virgin

Every Parrothead has to start with an initial Buffett concert and tailgate. Not counting children or teenagers who have been fortunate enough to go with their parents and families to shows, most Virgins (at least in terms of going to Buffett shows) are in their twenties or thirties. Typically, Virgins have listened to Jimmy Buffett's music and may even own *Songs You Know By Heart*. But until their first show, they haven't taken it to the next level, and they may not know quite what to expect.

For the most part, Virgins attend their first show with more experienced Parrotheads. Seasoned Vets help acclimate Virgins to the lay of the land, as far as tailgating protocol, games, drinking, and the actual concert go. The scene can be a little overwhelming to novices, so it helps to have those who've been there before to show them the ropes. And, assuming the Virgin survives the tailgating and the show, he or she can be truly considered a Parrothead.

The Cross-Dresser

Walking around the parking lot, you're sure to see a few guys who are really taking the tropical theme to heart. These are the Cross-Dressers—grown men voluntarily wearing coconut bras and grass skirts. While many of them are fairly innocuous, there are always a few whose bodily physique attracts extra notice—and they love it. For many of these brave men, the coconut

bra actually offers support, and the grass skirts brings attention to their overhanging beer bellies and plumber's cracks. But don't feel bad for them— these guys live for the attention such outrageous attire brings to them, and they happily stroll around the lot, looking for photo ops and greeting their public with a smile and an outstretched beer.

The Full-Time Parrothead

Full-Time Parrotheads are not too different from Seasoned Vets. They've been to more than their share of shows and tailgates and know the ropes. They have multiple Jimmy Buffett albums. So, what exactly sets Full-Time Parrotheads apart from the Seasoned Vets? For starters, they've followed the traveling circus, often catching multiple concerts on the same tour. Full-Timers won't just have the proper attire; they're also more likely to have a nine-foot inflatable shark and Parrothead signs to decorate their tailgates. A simple tailgate tent just won't do for Full-Timers; they'll have a full tiki-bar setup, complete with working electrical appliances and gourmet-quality cooking. Oftentimes, Full-Timers will bring an upscale portable toilet system, ensuring that they never have to pee with the masses. It's more than likely that these devoted folks have appeared in at least one of the Buffett video montages that are shown during concerts. And Full-Timers will also have plenty of stories about their favorite shows and memorable tailgating times.

The Family

Jimmy Buffett has been playing concerts for the masses for over thirty years. And many folks who have enjoyed his music and shows through time have passed on this way of life to younger generations of their sons, daughters, nieces, and nephews. It is by no means an unusual sight to see families, including younger children (called "Parakeets" by the Phlock), tailgating amongst the decadence and debauchery in the parking lot. Sure, the families, who are very much an accepted part of the tailgate scene, are probably not doing keg stands or body shots, but they enjoy themselves in their own way. Families are more apt to have their own impressive food spreads (complete with nonalcoholic beverages for the underage folks, of course). Adults, teenagers, and children alike may all dress up in Hawaiian shirts and grass skirts. They also play games such as Wiffle ball, Frisbee, and football.

The T.O. (Tailgate Only)

Finally, there are those folks who show up only for the partying before the show, without actually going to the concert. They are the T.O. (Tailgate Only) crowd. The T.O. may or may not have actually gone to a show in the past, but the T.O. certainly knows what a great time the Buffett tailgate is. They will show up with other Seasoned Vets or Full-Time Parrotheads and will take part in all the games and partying. The only difference is that when everyone packs up to go to the show, the T.O. will just hang around the parking lot for a while and continue the party there. Go to any Buffett show, and you will see that there are quite a few folks who fall into this category, which should be no surprise considering the appeal of the tailgating scene.

You Know You're a Parrothead When ...

- You have a Buffett album other than "Songs You Know By Heart."
- You own a Hawaiian shirt...or five.
- You have a hat in the shape of a parrot, cheeseburger, shark, or lobster.
- You start drinking before noon because "It's five o'clock somewhere..."

- You know who "Mr. Utley" is.
- You have a real license plate that reads "P-HEAD," "JIMMY," "BUFFETT," or "KEYWEST."
- You have a tattoo of some of the lyrics of "Margaritaville."
- You listen to Radio Margaritaville 24/7... and you know when the next live concert is being aired.
- You've done something that got you on the big screen at a Buffett concert.
- You own a coconut bra...and you're a guy.
- You have a display "Save the Manatee" license plate.

- You remember when Jimmy actually was a pirate looking at forty.
- You actually made yourself a "License to Chill."
- You think "Brown Eyed Girl" is a Buffett original.

Fruitcakes: How to Dress Like a Parrothead

If you're going to be hanging out in the land of the Parrotheads, you'll need to dress like one. When you're planning your tailgate wardrobe, think tropical and tacky. Neutral solids and tasteful duds will stick out like a sore thumb, while Hawaiian shirts and pink flamingos will blend right in with the wackiness. Mix and match from these costuming ideas:

The Perfect Hawaiian Shirt

This is the uniform of a Parrothead—cheery and colorful, with patterns of traditional flowers and palm trees or outrageous parrots and margaritas. Just looking at a Parrothead's shirt will put you in the tropical mood, dreaming of warm ocean breezes and mellow music. Women may also opt to wear a dress in a similar pattern.

Grass Skirts and Coconut Bras

Taking the Hawaiian theme one step further (and raising the tacky quotient a bit), some concertgoers choose to wear a grass skirt and a coconut bra, usually with shorts and a bikini top underneath. These two items can be worn in combination or separately, though a coconut bra without a grass skirt is more rare than the reverse. Look for a natural grass skirt—most Parrotheads wouldn't be caught dead in one of the bright green plastic versions. On a really hot day (or to show off your legs), consider trimming your grass skirt into a mini skirt.

Bikinis and Shorts

Taking advantage of the hot weather, many women prefer to show a little skin, wearing a bikini top and shorts. This outfit is appropriate for the beach theme and the usual temperature at the tailgate, but doesn't allow for as much creativity and personal expression as other costumes.

The Concert Tee

Some Parrotheads prefer to brag about their history of following the band by wearing Jimmy Buffett concert T-shirts from previous years. While these do not stand out as much as a loud Hawaiian shirt, they're the perfect solution for the slightly more dignified Parrothead who wants street cred.

Crazy Costumes

Want to really get noticed in the cacophony of over-the-top outfits? Wear a full costume to transform yourself into a pirate, a parrot, a margarita, or a lost shaker of salt. Creativity is key here, and the more unusual your costume, the more likely you'll get filmed for the "Changes in Latitudes" video montage.

Getting Lei'd

Wearing a lei, at least until it starts to get too hot, is a must. A colorful Hawaiian lei adds immediate impact and makes you feel like you've traveled to an exotic location. Most party supply catalogs sell a wide variety of leis, from cheap, basic ones to deluxe, full ones. If you prefer to keep your neck unencumbered, buy smaller wrist leis or wrap your regular-sized one around your wrist multiple times.

Beads & Bangles

A Buffett tailgate is often compared to being on Bourbon Street in New Orleans during Mardi Gras. Some of Bourbon Street's traditions have even

spilled over into the Buffett pre-party. Many tailgaters prefer to substitute Mardi Gras beads for Hawaiian leis, and you'll even see some women who are willing to flash people to acquire these beads. Invest in a Buffett-themed string of beads, with molded margarita or cheeseburger bangles and you'll get many offers from Parrotheads who'd like to earn your beads.

Hilarious Hats

Parrotheads are legendary for wearing ridiculous headgear, most of which are themed to honor their favorite Jimmy Buffett songs. In addition to providing a bit of personality to your outfit, a silly hat can help protect you from the sun. Look for Parrothead hats and visors at a party or costume store, or make your own. In a pinch, don a simple straw hat and loop a lei around the center.

Parrot: What could be more appropriate for a Parrothead than wearing a parrot on his or her head? It's easy to find felt parrot hats online or in stores. Or, start with a straw hat and attach a stuffed parrot toy or inflatable parrot to the center. Add a piece of Hawaiian fabric around the hat band and glue or sew fake flowers, feathers, beads, or other accessories to the rim.

Cheeseburger: Another fan favorite, "Cheeseburger in Paradise" has inspired countless commercially-made felt cheeseburger hats. This theme is more difficult to make at home, but if you're feeling ambitious, use felt and stuffing to sew a custom version.

Shark: Many Buffett fans have a strong affinity for "Fins." If you're one of them, choose from foam hats with a fin on top or felt hats featuring a shark chomping on the top of your head. Or, it's easy to make your own land shark creation from a straw hat, a fishing net, and an inflatable shark toy.

CHAPTER 3

Tailgating 101

Back to the Island: The Basics

There's an art to tailgating, and Parrotheads are the masters of that art.

Taking the day off work, they arrive at the parking lot before it opens, angling for the best spot. Towing portable tiki bars, pounds of sand, grills, and sundry other tailgating accessories, they make the Jimmy Buffett concert into an all-day experience. These devoted fans have all the comforts of home as they turn a plain parking lot into Margaritaville for the day.

A few of the cities that Jimmy Buffett typically hits just aren't set up for mass tailgating. But that doesn't mean the Parrotheads take it easy. Instead of setting up in the parking lots, they choose alternate venues for their pre-parties, attending a street party in front of the Margaritaville in Las Vegas or going to bars near Madison Square Garden in New York City, for example.

But the preferred way to enjoy the hours before the show is still the traditional tailgate. Longtime Parrotheads go all-out with incredible decorations and displays, but you can have a great time in the parking lot even without these amenities. Just make sure you have these Top 10 essential things needed for a successful Buffett tailgate.

1. **Sunscreen**—Always wear a broad-spectrum sunscreen, and reapply often.

2. **Water**—Drink a glass of water after each alcoholic drink, and you'll last all the way to the encore.

3. **Sunglasses**—Your eyes need sun protection too, so bring a fun pair with UVA and UVB protection.

4. **Hat**—Those straw hats and parrot visors aren't just fashion statements, they'll help you keep your cool.

5. **Chair**—There's nothing better than sipping a margarita while relaxing in a comfortable chair.

6. **Table**—A table is a good place to place your food, drinks, and decorations as well as a necessity for games such as beer pong and flip cup.

7. **Coolers**—You need to keep those beverages and frozen food cold.

8. **Grill**—Burgers, hot dogs, and grilled chicken are standard fare at tailgates.

9. **Tent or umbrella**—From time to time, you'll need to take shelter from the sun and heat.

10. **Margaritas**—A Buffett tailgate isn't complete without them.

The Police Presence

Police officers are your friends, especially during tailgates. They will patrol the parking lots, often on bicycles, to ensure that everyone stays safe and out of potential trouble. As alcoholic beverages are generally permitted during Buffett shows, the officers are not looking to arrest everyone with an open container of alcohol. Instead, they want to make sure everyone has a good time and that no one is doing anything dangerous. As long as you do what the cops tell you to do, they'll basically leave you alone. They know what to expect, and most of them probably volunteered for Buffett duty.

Additionally, the police officers offer a necessary service. If a tailgater is experiencing heat stroke or dehydration, officers may offer the tailgater the chance to cool off in a police cruiser, call for emergency assistance, or direct the victim to the nearest first aid station.

The key to having a positive experience with the cops is to acknowledge and befriend them when they pass by in the parking lot. Some folks offer leis and nonalcoholic beverages to them as gestures of goodwill. Many Parrotheads make it a point to get a photograph of themselves with the cops wearing leis.

Why It Might Be a Good Idea to Rent a Vehicle

Why worry about multiple people having to drive to the show when you can join the growing legions who roll up in their own private bus or recreational vehicle. Buses and RVs offer countless advantages: large capacity to transport groups and friends; a centralized location for groups to meet; an area to cool off and take shelter from the heat; and, perhaps most importantly, restroom access. For those who do not personally own a bus or RV, there are several options.

The Jimmy Buffett Concert Handbook

Local Parrothead clubs often advertise chartered trips in advance of a concert. Several companies offer short term RV rentals. Check out RV Rentals. net (www.rv-rentals.net), which lists various RV rental companies in different regions. Cruise America (www.cruiseamerica.com) is another national RV rental company. As far as buses, BusRates.com (www.busrates.com) is one resource that lists companies that charter buses for short term rental. When enough people chip in to defray the rental costs, the rate is not prohibitive, and the burden is well worth the benefits.

A Guide to Portable Bathrooms

When you're sitting in the parking lot drinking all day (whether it's margaritas or water), you'll eventually have to answer nature's call. Finding a toilet that isn't completely disgusting is of primary importance, and planning ahead can help a lot. However, as the day goes on, your preferred bathroom type may change as the conditions (and your condition) change. Keep these hints in mind to stay as sanitary and sane as possible when you have to pee.

Public Toilets

Most concert venues that are expecting large numbers of Buffett tailgaters will rent portable public toilets for the parking lots. They are usually lined up along one edge of the parking lot or grouped in smaller clusters in the corners of the lots. Whatever you call them— Porta-Potties, the Head, Porta-Johns—these plastic latrines are distinctly more pleasant earlier in the day, before legions of drunk people use and abuse them. Most run out of toilet paper quickly and do not have hand-wash stations, so bring tissues or toilet paper and a hand sanitizer with you to cleanup afterward.

Bus/RV Bathrooms

Having access to a bus or RV bathroom at a Buffett tailgate can seem almost luxurious. After all, it's a private, indoor bathroom theoretically restricted to use by people you know (or just met). Recreational vehicles in particular may have a sink for washing your hands—a big advantage over all the other parking lot bathroom choices. Even if you don't have direct access to a bus or RV, you may still be able to take advantage of these perks by finding people you know who came in one. Some groups allow friends to use

their facilities for a small fee, or use your shared love of all things Buffett to charm your way into a fellow Parrothead's potty. As a last resort, you can always look for a disorganized chartered bus gathering where not everyone knows each other, and sneak on board for the bathroom.

Camp Potty

Many experienced tailgaters invest in a portable camping toilet with a curtain around it. This allows for more control over your bathroom experience, but can also be a pain when it comes time to dispose of the waste. It also requires a bit of setup to hang the curtain. Camp toilets can be as simple as a plastic rim suspended over a large plastic bag for around $15, or as deluxe as a flushing toilet for $100. Either way, you can be sure that you'll have a consistent, clean toilet with no line.

Between the Cars

It's half an hour before the show, and you're a half-mile walk from the concert venue. You and everyone else in the parking lot really have to pee, and the lines for the Porta-Potties are ridiculous. What are you going to do? As unpleasant as it may sound, many people in this situation opt for finding as much privacy as possible between the opened doors of two parked cars. However, you can avoid this time crunch if you plan ahead—always make your last bathroom run at least an hour to an hour and a half before the show.

Keeping Cool in the Heat

Most Buffett tour dates take place during the summer months, and those dates that fall outside the summer are usually for year-round warm-weather climates such as Hawaii, Southern California, and Florida. For folks tailgating for hours on end in the heat, keeping cool and hydrated are key. After all, it really isn't any fun to be in the first aid center or hospital right during the concert. Besides the routine methods, there are some ways of staying cool that really epitomize the Buffett lifestyle.

Fluids

Drinking lots of fluids (preferably water) is an essential. As a guideline, try to drink at least one nonalcoholic beverage after every one to two alcoholic ones, and you'll survive through the encore.

Shelter

Tailgaters frequently duck out of the sun by going under a tent, canopy, or umbrella, or into an air-conditioned vehicle. The open back hatch of a minivan can provide some shade and act as a staging area for your party. Or, set up a large tent shelter and be the envy of your tailgating neighbors. (Putting your cooler in the shade also helps the drinks stay cold longer.)

Baby Pool

Bring along a baby wading pool and fill it with cold water or bags of ice. The ice will naturally melt from the heat, and people can set up chairs around the pool to wade in and provide enjoyable relief for one's feet. Or, if the pool is big enough, people can just jump right in and sit in the pool.

Water Guns

Bring a water gun if you have one. In the hot sun, a nice spray from a water gun feels pretty good. It's not uncommon to see water gun "fights," where everyone wins. Try filling several water guns with water and keeping them in the cooler until you're ready to spray.

First Aid for the Phlock

Almost every Buffett tailgater will experience some kind of sun- or heat-related illness, whether it's a mild case of sunburn or a heat stroke emergency. Knowing how to identify the symptoms early and treat them before they get worse can keep you in the parking lot having fun instead of at the hospital.

The following are a few of the most common illnesses you might encounter at a Buffett tailgate and advice on how to treat them. However, if you feel worse than you seem to others, your symptoms grow rapidly worse, or your heart rate or breathing changes, you should seek help from an emergency medical technician immediately. At most Buffett tailgates, they drive around the parking lots in golf carts or can be summoned quickly by police officers.

Dehydration

This one's easy to recognize—if you feel thirsty, tired, or light-headed, have dry skin, or don't need to pee as much as you should, you're probably dehydrated. Drinking alcoholic or caffeinated beverages and standing outside in the heat all day are two major causes of dehydration at Buffett shows. To prevent dehydration, drink plenty of water and sports drinks throughout the day. Spend some time in the shade so that you're not sweating away all your fluids. If the dehydration is severe, contact an emergency medical technician immediately, as you might need intravenous fluids to restore your fluid levels.

Sunburn

A sunburn may not seem like a big deal, but the long hours spent in the sun at a Buffett tailgate can easily turn into a blistering second-degree burn. The symptoms of a second-degree sunburn include blisters, swelling, headaches, or fever. If you have sunburn, you should immediately move to the shade or cover the area with clothing to prevent further damage. When you get home, use soap to wash off any impurities that may be blocking your pores and inhibiting the body's natural cooling process. If you do have a more serious second-degree burn, apply dry, sterile dressings to the blisters and seek medical attention. Sunburn can be easily prevented by staying out of the sun, reapplying broad-spectrum sunscreen on your skin about every two hours, and wearing a wide-brimmed hat.

The Jimmy Buffett Concert Handbook

Heat Exhaustion

If you and your friends have been standing outside in the heat for several hours, be on the lookout for the symptoms of heat exhaustion. A person with heat exhaustion may have skin that feels cold or looks either pale or flushed; the person may have a headache or feel nauseous or dizzy; or the person may feel unnaturally weak or exhausted. If you suspect someone has heat exhaustion, move the person to an air-conditioned car, or get the person into the shade and fan him or her. Loosen the person's clothing and apply cool, wet towels or cloths to his or her skin. If the person is conscious, give him or her small amounts of cool water to sip. If the person vomits, becomes unconscious, or worsens, seek help from the emergency medical technicians immediately.

Heat Stroke

Heat stroke is a severe heat-related illness that should be treated as an emergency. It often begins as a case of heat exhaustion that is not treated and worsens. The symptoms of heat stroke include red skin that can be either dry or moist, rapid, shallow breathing, a rapid, weak pulse, or unconsciousness. If you encounter a person with any these symptoms, you should immediately seek emergency medical help. While you wait for help to arrive, move the person to an air-conditioned car, or get the person into the shade and fan him or her. Loosen the person's clothing and apply cool, wet towels or cloths to his or her skin.

Alcohol Poisoning

Most Parrotheads know how to party without taking it too far, but occasionally the combination of heat and heavy drinking result in alcohol poisoning. This serious (and sometimes deadly) illness results from drinking too much alcohol in a short time, and dehydration can make it worse. If you see someone at the tailgate who is vomiting, has slow or irregular breathing, has very pale or bluish skin, seems very confused, or has passed out, seek emergency medical assistance immediately. Don't leave the person alone, and do not try to make them vomit. To help prevent alcohol poisoning, drink slowly and in moderation. Alternate between alcoholic beverages and water and be sure to eat during the day.

One Particular Harbour:
Decorating Tips for Tailgates

Once you have the basics of the tailgate down, it's time to start adding some Parrothead flavor to your experience. A little advance planning will help you enjoy the laid-back atmosphere of the pre-party without stress.

The main ingredients in creating your own little slice of paradise in the parking lot are to set the mood with fun decorations, bring plenty of tasty treats (both liquid and solid), and plan some light entertainment.

First, transform your parking space into a mini Margaritaville or a day at the beach. Simply choose your favorite Buffett song or songs, and decorate accordingly. Feel free to mix and match themes—Parrotheads aren't particular. (Just be sure the decorations are safe, particularly when you're embellishing your car.)

The following are some basic decorating ideas, which can be customized for specific themes.

- Look for inflatable decorations at party stores, or substitute inflatable water toys, which are conveniently made in beach themes.
- Tie appropriate helium balloons to your car or shelter.
- Printed paper decorations can add a lot of flair with little expense and no wasted room.
  - Cut out face holes in a large piece of plywood and paint outrageous characters on the front (like a ukulele-playing, bikini-clad woman or a pirate).
  - When in doubt, go tacky— a Buffett tailgate is the one place where tacky is cool.

Tropical Paradise

If you can't go to the tropics, bring the tropics to you by decorating your car and parking space like a beach. Inflatable palm trees can be tied to the car luggage rack or the corners of your shelter to immediately set the mood. Paint the car windows with more palm trees (perhaps with a hammock between them) and laid-back sayings such as "We are the people our parents warned us about," "License to chill," and "It's five o'clock somewhere." To customize your tropical paradise even more, consider these additions:

- Tape grass skirts around the outside of your vehicle so they just brush the ground.
- Bring a freestanding hammock.
- Buy enough sand to make a small beach in the parking lot.
- Fill an inflatable pool with water and put it in the middle of your beach.
- Hang stuffed parrots around your area (some diehards have even been spotted with a real parrot at the tailgate!)
- Set up a limbo bar and watch the Parrotheads line up.
- Buy a portable bamboo tiki bar from a party supply catalog, or build your own, complete with grass roof, signage, and stools for patrons.

Margaritaville Madness

Create your own oasis of Margaritaville in which to enjoy your margaritas. It's easy to paint your car windows with images of margarita glasses, salt shakers, limes, and such. Include a few phrases from the song, such as "Wastin' away again" and "Lost shaker of salt." You can also add some of these larger decorations:

- Tie inflatable cacti to your shelter.
- Contact your local Cuervo or other tequila distributor to see if you can get one of the temporary signs they give to bars. Customize it with song lyrics.
- Buy or rent a giant inflatable margarita glass.

Land Sharks

Turn your car into a land shark in honor of "Fins." The easiest way is to buy a heavy-duty inflatable shark water toy and tie it securely to the luggage rack on your roof. Then, paint "Fins up!" and "Fins to the left, fins to the right!" on your car windows, along with some waves and fins. For a more professional touch, try these ideas:

- Put a fishing net over your car hood.
- Stuff the head of a stuffed shark toy through

your car's front grill so that it looks like it ran into you.

- If you can find or build one, attach a gaping shark's mouth to the front or back of your car, or tie a giant fin to the roof. You can also build a giant plywood shark's tail for the back of your car.

Parking Lot Pirates

If you're the type of person who appreciates the slightly subversive aspect of being a Parrothead, you're a natural pirate. Paint a few skull and crossbones on your car window, fly the Jolly Roger from your car antenna or hang it from your shelter, and add some of these special touches:

- Paint pirates saying things like "Arrgh!" and "Shiver me timbers!" on your car window.
- Write "A pirate looks at" and your age on the window.
- Turn your pickup truck into a pirate ship with square sails and a basket as the lookout.

Run It Up the Flagpole

Okay, so you've got a prime tailgating spot and you've decorated it to the nines. But in the crush of cars and people, your Parrothead friends can't find your little spot of heaven despite your best attempt at giving directions. There's a simple solution to this age-old problem: bring a flagpole. The key to making this work, however, is coming up with your own unique combination of "flags." Popular flags include the skull and crossbones, an inflatable shark, or even bras collected from passersby.

Cheeseburger in Paradise: Food for the Phlock

Great food is an essential part of any Buffett tailgate. After all, Jimmy's songs have spawned two restaurant chains and countless cheeseburger hats. If you're not into cooking in the parking lot, you can take the

easy way out and bring hoagies. Most Parrotheads opt to grill some cheeseburgers, hot dogs, or chicken instead—it's easy to do and much more satisfying after a long day of celebrating.

Tailgate Grilling

In recent years, many tailgaters have started to switch over to the new breed of portable propane grills, which make grilling a snap. They light instantly and leave none of that nasty ash cleanup. However, if you're still using an old-school charcoal grill, follow these instructions to build the best batch of hot coals.

Lighting Charcoal

Before you begin to light your fire, have a fire extinguisher or bucket of water on hand in case of emergency. A charcoal chimney starter is the best way to start a charcoal fire. With a charcoal chimney, there's no need to use lighter fluid, which can make your food

taste funny. Simply fill the larger part of the chimney with charcoal. Place a fire-starter or twisted paper and small twigs on the ground, and set the chimney on top. Using a match, light the firestarter or paper. If the paper starts to burn out, add more paper or twigs until the coals catch well. The coals will catch on fire and send flames up through the top of the chimney. Once the flames have receded and the coals are glowing red with white ash around the outside, carefully pour the hot coals into the base of the charcoal grill.

If you don't have a charcoal chimney, pour the charcoal into the base of the grill. Twist some paper and place it in the center of your grill, then stack the charcoal around and above it in a loose pyramid shape. Be sure to leave some space for airflow. Once the

pyramid is built, carefully sprinkle a small amount of lighter fluid over the coals. Place the lighter fluid bottle away from the grill. Light a match and toss it into the pyramid so that it catches the paper and lighter fluid on fire. Even after the lighter fluid burns off, the coals should continue to smoke and feel warm. Once most of them are glowing red with white ash on the outside, use a tool to spread them out.

Putting the Fire Out

The hardest part about grilling before a Buffett concert is putting the charcoal out before the show. Many people simply pour the charcoals onto the ground, but this can be hazardous to people walking or driving by. First, put the cover on the grill with the vents closed to help the coals burn out. To help speed them along, you can sprinkle them with water, a little at a time, stirring the coals to expose hot spots. Once you can hold the palm of your hand above the coals without feeling any warmth, the fire is out. It's not a good idea to pour a lot of water over the coals, as this creates a big mess and can cause sparks or hot steam to burn you.

Now that you have something to cook the food on, try one of these favorite recipes:

A Cheeseburger That Tastes Like Paradise

Every bite of these seasoned, cheesy burgers will make you think you're in paradise. Mixing the shredded cheese into the meat keeps the beef moist and gives the burger a great crunchy exterior. For a noncheese burger, simply skip the shredded cheese. Makes 8 quarter-pound cheeseburgers.

- ✿ 2 pounds ground beef (80 to 85 percent lean)
- ✿ 1 teaspoon Worcestershire sauce
- ✿ ½ teaspoon onion powder
- ✿ ½ teaspoon garlic salt
- ✿ ½ teaspoon celery salt
- ✿ ½ teaspoon kosher salt
- ✿ ¼ teaspoon freshly ground pepper
- ✿ 2 cups shredded cheddar cheese
- ✿ 8 hamburger buns

1. Place the ground beef in a large bowl. Sprinkle the Worcestershire sauce, onion powder, garlic salt, celery salt, kosher salt, and pepper over the beef.

2. Using your fingers, gently knead the seasonings into the beef until they are just barely mixed in, being careful not to overwork the meat.

3. Divide the meat into 8 equal sections. Working the meat as little as possible, form each portion into a ball, and then pat it flat to form a hamburger patty about ¾-inch thick. Gently press the center of each patty to create a slight dent, making it a little thinner in the center than it is on the edges.

4. Place the patties in a resealable plastic container, separated by sheets of aluminum foil, and store in a refrigerator or cooler until ready to cook.

5. Grill the burgers over hot coals until well-seared (about 5 minutes per side), flipping once with a spatula.

6. Serve on a toasted hamburger bun with desired condiments.

Sausage with Sauerkraut

Grilled sausages are the classic tailgating food. Easy to cook, hard to mess up, and supremely satisfying after a long afternoon in Margaritaville, these juicy dogs are sure to please. Makes 8 sausages.

- ✿ 1 bag sauerkraut
- ✿ 8 precooked sausages or hot dogs
- ✿ 8 hot dog buns

1. Fold a large piece of heavy-duty aluminum foil in half. Place the sauerkraut in the middle of the foil. Bring two opposite edges of the foil together and fold them over twice, leaving room for steam. Fold each of the two remaining

edges over twice separately to close the sides of the pouch. Place in the middle of a hot grill.

2. Place the sausages around the foil package and grill them over hot coals for about 8 to 10 minutes. To avoid flare-ups and keep the sausages juicy, do not prick or slice them before placing them on the grill. Frequently turn the sausages with tongs to cook them evenly.

3. Remove the sauerkraut package from the grill and open it carefully, avoiding any steam that escapes.

4. Place one sausage on a bun, then cover with sauerkraut.

Jamaican Jerk Chicken

Jimmy Buffett got shot out of the sky trying to reach some of this Jamaican delicacy. We like to brighten up a commercially bottled sauce with a few fresh ingredients. Try it for yourself, and see why Buffett was willing to risk his life for this spicy chicken recipe. Makes 8 chicken breast cutlets.

- ❀ 1 cup bottled Jamaican jerk sauce
- ❀ ¼ cup fresh lemon juice
- ❀ 1 onion, sliced lengthwise

- ✿ 2 garlic cloves, minced or pressed
- ✿ 8 chicken breast cutlets

1. Combine the jerk sauce, lemon juice, onion, garlic, and chicken in a large zip-top plastic bag. Marinate in the refrigerator overnight, turning occasionally. Store in a cooler until ready to cook.

2. Remove the chicken from the bag, discarding marinade. Grill the chicken over hot coals for 10 minutes or until done, turning once.

Boat Drinks

You'll definitely want to wet your whistle while you're standing around the parking lot all afternoon. Beer and soda are fine for a traditional football tailgate, but with Jimmy Buffett's emphasis on island living, you'll want the kinds of fancy drinks that they serve at tropical resorts. You know, the ones with the little umbrellas and a fruit garnish? This is a perfect time to plan ahead, as many of these recipes can be made a day or two before the concert and frozen. Simply pack them in your cooler and enjoy the frosty goodness with little work.

However, for piña coladas, banana daiquiris, and all of the mocktails, you'll need a working blender. Thankfully, you won't need a monster of an extension cord—there are tailgating blenders on the market that use a battery that can be recharged using your car's cigarette lighter and others that run on gas. There have even been sightings of gas-powered blenders mounted on Segways to form a tiki bar on the go at several Buffett tailgates.

Margaritas

Margaritas for a Crowd

Margaritas are the essential drink for any Jimmy Buffett event. But who wants to sit around making them all day when you could be hanging out and having fun? Preparing these margaritas ahead of time and storing them in your fridge or cooler in plastic gallon jugs will keep you wastin' away again instead of working away in Margaritaville. They're perfectly portable and ready to pour over ice. Makes about 2 gallons.

- ✿ 4 (12-ounce) cans limeade concentrate
- ✿ 1 cup fresh lime juice (or bottled Real Lime)
- ✿ 3 quarts water
- ✿ 1 fifth (750 mL) tequila
- ✿ 1 pint triple sec
- ✿ Lime wedges
- ✿ Kosher salt

1. In a large bowl, combine the limeade, lime juice, water, tequila, and triple sec. Stir to mix well.
2. Pour the mixture into empty water jugs or a large drink cooler. Keep the mixture cool in a refrigerator or cooler.

3. Prepare the cups by rubbing a lime wedge around the lip of each cup. Pour kosher salt onto a small plate and roll the outer edge of the lip in the salt.

4. To serve, fill the cup with ice cubes. Pour the margaritas over the ice and garnish with a lime wedge.

Make-Ahead Frozen Margaritas

There's no need for a blender with these super-simple frozen margaritas. Simply make the recipe at room temperature and freeze—then scrape some margarita slush into your cup! A good cooler will keep these frozen for several hours in the parking lot—and they're particularly refreshing on a hot summer day. Makes about 2 gallons.

- ❀ 4 (12-ounce) cans limeade concentrate
- ❀ 1 cup fresh lime juice (or bottled Real Lime)
- ❀ 3½ quarts water
- ❀ 1 fifth (750 mL) tequila
- ❀ 1 pint triple sec
- ❀ Lime wedges
- ❀ Kosher salt

1. Pour the limeade, lime juice, tequila, triple sec, and water into a large bowl. Stir until well mixed.

2. Ladle the mixture into freezable containers such as Glad Ware, filling them not-quite full. Seal the containers and freeze for at least 24 hours.

3. Transport the margarita containers to the tailgate in a good cooler packed with ice.

4. Prepare the cups by rubbing a lime wedge around the lip of each cup. Pour kosher salt onto a small plate and roll the outer edge of the lip in the salt.

5. To serve, use a large metal spoon to scrape the margaritas into cups. The margaritas should be roughly the texture of water ice or sorbet. Garnish with a lime wedge and serve with a spoon. Return remaining margarita to the freezer or cooler.

Strawberry Margaritas

Are classic margaritas too sour for your liking? Blend in some sweet strawberries for a delightful concoction that'll leave you wanting more. This recipe might even convert those who usually sneer at fruity drinks. Makes 1 gallon.

- ✿ 6 ounces frozen strawberries
- ✿ 6 cups water, separated
- ✿ 2 (12-ounce) cans limeade concentrate
- ✿ ½ cup fresh lime juice (or bottled Real Lime)
- ✿ 1½ cups tequila
- ✿ 1 cup triple sec
- ✿ Lime wedges
- ✿ Granulated sugar
- ✿ Fresh strawberries, to garnish (optional)

1. In a blender, combine the strawberries and 2 cups of the water. Blend until smooth. Pour into a large bowl.
2. Add the limeade, lime juice, tequila, triple sec, and remaining 4 cups of water to the bowl. Stir until well mixed.

3. Ladle the mixture into freezable containers such as Glad Ware, filling them not-quite full. Seal the containers and freeze for at least 24 hours.

4. Transport the margarita containers to the tailgate in a good cooler packed with ice.

5. Prepare the cups by rubbing a lime wedge around the lip of each cup. Pour granulated sugar onto a small plate and roll the outer edge of the lip in the sugar.

6. To serve, use a large metal spoon to scrape the margaritas into cups. The margaritas should be roughly the texture of water ice or sorbet. Garnish with a strawberry or lime wedge and serve with a spoon. Return remaining margarita to the freezer or cooler.

Mango Margaritas

What do you get when you take the Last Mango in Paris to Margaritaville? This tasty tropical treat! Makes 1 gallon.

- ✿ 1 (12-ounce) bag frozen mango slices
- ✿ ½ cup mango nectar
- ✿ 6 cups water, separated
- ✿ 2 (12-ounce) cans limeade concentrate
- ✿ ½ cup fresh lime juice (or bottled Real Lime)
- ✿ 1½ cups tequila
- ✿ 1 cup triple sec
- ✿ Lime wedges
- ✿ Kosher salt
- ✿ Fresh mango slices, to garnish (optional)

1. In a blender, combine the mango slices, mango nectar, and 2 cups of the water. Blend until smooth. Pour into a large bowl.
2. Add the limeade, lime juice, tequila, triple sec, and remaining 4 cups of water to the bowl. Stir until well mixed.
3. Ladle the mixture into freezable containers such as Glad Ware, filling them not-quite full. Seal the containers and freeze for at least 24 hours.

4. Transport the margarita containers to the tailgate in a good cooler packed with ice.

5. Prepare the cups by rubbing a lime wedge around the lip of each cup. Pour granulated sugar onto a small plate and roll the outer edge of the lip in the sugar.

6. To serve, use a large metal spoon to scrape the margaritas into cups. The margaritas should be roughly the texture of water ice or sorbet. Garnish with a mango slice or a lime wedge and serve with a spoon. Return remaining margarita to the freezer or cooler.

Other Tropical Favorites

Make-Ahead Frozen Strawberry Daiquiris

These strawberry daiquiris are easy to make, and even easier to eat! Simply mix them at room temperature and store overnight in the freezer. The alcohol prevents the liquid from freezing completely, leaving you to scrape the slush into your cup. Makes 1 gallon.

- ✿ 1 (12 ounce) bag frozen strawberries
- ✿ 4 cups water, separated
- ✿ 1 (12 ounce) can frozen limeade concentrate, thawed
- ✿ 1 (12 ounce) can frozen lemonade concentrate, thawed
- ✿ 1 pint light rum

1. In a blender, combine the strawberries and 2 cups of the water. Blend until smooth. Pour into a large bowl.
2. Add the remaining water, the limeade, the lemonade, and the rum to the bowl. Stir until well mixed.
3. Ladle the mixture into freezable containers such as Glad Ware, filling them not-quite full. Seal the containers and freeze for at least 24 hours.

4. Transport the daiquiri containers to the tail-gate in a good cooler packed with ice.

5. To serve, use a large metal spoon to scrape the daiquiris into cups. The daiquiris should be roughly the texture of water ice or sorbet. Garnish with a strawberry or lime wedge and serve with a spoon. Return remaining daiquiri to the freezer or cooler.

Banana Daiquiris

Blended bananas give this daiquiri a smooth, creamy texture. Makes about 4 servings.

- ✿ 4 bananas
- ✿ 8 ounces limeade concentrate, thawed
- ✿ 1 cup light rum
- ✿ 4 cups ice cubes
- ✿ Maraschino cherries, to garnish

1. Peel the bananas and break into several pieces.

2. Combine the bananas, limeade, rum, and ice in an electric blender. Pulse on low speed until the ice has disappeared, then blend on high speed until smooth.

3. Pour the daiquiris into 4 cups and garnish each with a maraschino cherry.

Piña Coladas

Literally meaning "strained pineapple," the piña colada has evolved over the years into a delicious blend of tropical treats—pineapple, coconut cream, and rum. A maraschino cherry and a pineapple slice make the perfect garnish. Makes about 6 servings.

- ❀ 1 (8½ ounce) can cream of coconut
- ❀ 1½ cups pineapple juice
- ❀ 1 (8 ounce) can crushed pineapple
- ❀ 1½ cups light rum
- ❀ 6 cups ice cubes
- ❀ Fresh pineapple slices, to garnish
- ❀ Maraschino cherries, to garnish

1. Combine the cream of coconut, pineapple juice, crushed pineapple, and rum in an electric blender. Blend until smooth.
2. Add the ice and blend until thick but smooth.
3. Pour into cups and garnish with a pineapple slice and a maraschino cherry skewered on a cocktail sword.

Chelada

On a hot summer day, add a refreshing twist to your basic beer with this simple, Mexican-inspired recipe. A chelada is best served like a margarita—on the rocks in a glass rimmed with salt. Makes 1 chelada.

- ½ lime
- Kosher salt
- Ice cubes
- 1 bottle or can of light lager beer

1. Rub the lime half around the outer lip of the cup.
2. Pour the salt onto a small plate. Roll the outer lip of the cup in the salt.
3. Squeeze the lime half into the cup, extracting about 1 ounce of juice.
4. Fill the cup with ice cubes and slowly pour the beer over the ice, trying to minimize the foam.

Mocktails

Frozen Mock-aritas

Can't drink the hard stuff? You can still enjoy an afternoon in Margaritaville with these nonalcoholic frozen margaritas. Makes 4 servings.

- ❀ 1 (12 ounce) can frozen limeade concentrate, thawed
- ❀ ½ cup orange juice
- ❀ ¼ cup water
- ❀ 4 cups ice cubes
- ❀ Lime wedges
- ❀ Kosher salt

1. Combine the limeade, orange juice, water, and ice in an electric blender. Pulse on low spend, then blend on high speed until the ice cubes are crushed.
2. Prepare the cups by rubbing a lime wedge around the lip of each cup. Pour kosher salt onto a small plate and roll the outer edge of the lip in the salt.
3. Pour the mock-aritas into the cups and garnish with lime wedges.

Virgin Strawberry Daiquiris

These nonalcoholic strawberry daiquiris are fast and easy to make, and the tang of fresh ingredients makes up for the missing rum. Makes 4 servings.

- ✿ 1 cup fresh strawberries, cored
- ✿ Juice of 4 limes
- ✿ 4 tablespoons sugar
- ✿ 4 cups ice cubes

1. Combine the strawberries, lime juice, and sugar in an electric blender. Pulse on low speed until the mixture is smooth.
2. Add ice cubes to the 4 cup mark on the blender. Blend until the mixture is smooth and the ice fully incorporated.
3. Pour the daiquiris into 4 cups and garnish each with a strawberry.

Mock Piña Coladas

Replace a piña colada's rum with rum extract and crushed pineapple, and you've got these mocktails that may just taste better than the real thing. Look for rum extract in the baking aisle of your grocery store. Makes about 6 servings.

- ❀ 1 (8½ ounce) can cream of coconut
- ❀ 1½ cups pineapple juice
- ❀ 1 (8 ounce) can crushed pineapple
- ❀ ½ teaspoon imitation rum extract
- ❀ 6 cups ice cubes
- ❀ Fresh pineapple slices, to garnish
- ❀ Maraschino cherries, to garnish

1. Combine the cream of coconut, pineapple juice, crushed pineapple, and rum extract in an electric blender. Blend until smooth.
2. Add the ice and blend until thick but smooth.
3. Pour into cups and garnish with a pineapple slice and a maraschino cherry skewered on a cocktail sword.

(Not-So) Quietly Making Noise: Your Tailgate Soundtrack

What would a Buffett tailgate be without the Buffett? Unless you're located near one of the larger parties that's blasting music, complete with a DJ, you'll want your own source of sound. Opening your car doors and playing your car stereo is one way of achieving this. But if you'd prefer to provide a soundtrack for your neighbors, you might want to invest in a portable power inverter that will allow you to use your car's battery to power a larger portable stereo system.

Top 10 Non-Buffett Bands to Play at Your Tailgate

You'll definitely hear some Jimmy Buffett tunes in the parking lot, but even Radio Margaritaville plays a lot of similarly themed songs by other artists. Try these other musicians who are often covered by Buffett or played by Radio Margaritaville when you need a break from the norm:

1. Bob Marley & the Wailers
2. Jack Johnson
3. Club Trini
4. Alan Jackson
5. Mac McAnally
6. The Eagles
7. Santana
8. Garth Brooks
9. Grateful Dead
10. Bruce Springsteen

License to Chill:
Games for Parrotheads

Looking for a way to wile away the hours until the concert? Try these games and welcome your neighbors to join in!

Frisbee Bowling

Who doesn't love to throw a Frisbee around? Frisbees flying through the air are a common sight at Buffett tailgates. Sometimes, though, the open space in the parking lot is reduced by tailgate set-ups and wandering Parrotheads, so some folks have taken to playing a more confined game of Frisbee bowling. With this game, there's a lot less risk of an errant throw smacking someone in the face. Instead, the risk is an off-target throw hitting someone in the ankle, but whomever you hit will probably not be as upset with you (especially if you offer the injured party a beer).

What You Need to Play

- Frisbee
- Makeshift pins in the way of empty plastic bottles or small plastic cones

Game Setup

Place the bottles or cones in a triangle as you would set up bowling pins.

Game Play

Standing about 10–15 feet away, throw the Frisbee at a low angle to try to knock over as many of the "pins" as possible. After the pins that have been knocked over are cleared, the player has a second opportunity to try to knock over the remaining obstacles. Then the other player has his or her turn. Score isn't always kept, as knocking over the bottles and cones is often satisfaction enough.

Wiffle Ball

Wiffle ball, of course, is a game many played in grade school. But as the song title goes, sometimes we're "growing older but not up." There won't be too many

full-fledged games in the parking lot, but there will often be folks taking swings with at a Wiffle ball with the standard Wiffle ball bat and a chair as a backstop. As the ball and bat are made of plastic, Wiffle ball is safe for play even in the parking lot. In this version, though we're really just taking batting practice, since it'd be difficult to run the bases in a busy parking lot.

What You Need to Play

- Plastic Wiffle ball and Wiffle ball bat
- A beach chair or similarly sized object to act as a backstop
- People willing to field the ball

Game Setup

Set up the chair as the backstop and target for the pitcher.

Game Play

Attempt to hit the plastic ball with a swing of the bat. Any ball that hits the chair or backstop on the fly is a strike. A swing and a miss is also a strike. After a determined number of strikes, someone else takes his or her turn at bat.

Football

Football: the current American pastime. And what tailgating scene, at either a sporting event or concert, would be complete without seeing footballs thrown about? Like Wiffle ball, there's usually not enough room for a full pickup game, so tailgaters usually just throw the ball around for fun.

Hacky Sack

Hacky Sack, or footbag, is a fun, friendly game in the parking lot, at least for those with good foot-eye coordination. A footbag is a small beanbag or sand bag that serves as a ball. Typically, those taking part (3–5 works best) form a circle and attempt to kick and pass it to each other without using their hands and without letting it hit the ground. It's a friendly game, because those kicking the footbag around are usually welcoming of random strangers who want to join in (provided that the newcomers are respectful of proper etiquette, such as passing it around so everyone has a chance to kick it, picking up the footbag if you caused it to hit the ground, etc.). For those who become good at it, kicking a footbag around is quite relaxing and fun.

Limbo

More of a dance than a game, limbo actually originated in the Caribbean on the island of Trinidad. With this legacy, it is only natural that folks will "do the limbo" while Buffett music or other similar rhythms are played in the background.

What You Need to Play

- A long stick, such as a broom stick
- Two limbo poles with places to hold the limbo

stick at different heights, or two volunteers to hold it

- Caribbean music
- A line of limbo dancers

Game Setup

Set the two poles (or your volunteers) in an open area. Put the limbo stick at the highest setting or have your volunteers hold it at shoulder height. Turn the music on.

Game Play

Each person dances to the music and approaches the limbo stick. As you reach the stick, lean backward and dance under the horizontal stick without touching it. If you touch it, you're out of the contest. If you make it safely through, you go to the end of the line. When the first person gets back to the head of the line, the stick is lowered. It gets lower and lower until only one dancer remains.

Tricycle Races

Tricycle races—yes, tricycle races—are more common in the parking lot than one would think. Maybe because so much of being a Parrothead is about not growing up, riding a tricycle fits right in. Factor in drinking beer before the race and you have what amounts to socially acceptable (well, at least in the parking lot) drinking and driving. And you'd be surprised by how difficult it is to ride a kid's tricycle when you're fully grown.

What You Need to Play

- Two or more tricycles
- Beer or other beverage (optional)

Game Play

Before racing, the participants can choose to drink, which, theoretically, impairs their performance. Then, they ride the tricycles up the parking lot, possibly through obstacles, to a determined finish line. Much cheering from neighboring tailgates and wandering bystanders ensues.

Flip Cup

Flip cup is a game that has grown in popularity in recent years at tailgates. For the uninitiated, flip cup is essentially a drinking relay race between two teams of equal numbers of people, usually 2–6. Some of the appeal of flip cup is that a lot of people can participate in one game and it is easy to learn how to play.

What You Need to Play

- Plastic cups
- A table that is long enough to handle the number of people playing
- Beer or other beverage for the cups

Game Setup

The teams stand on opposite sides of a table facing a counterpart from the other team across the table. Each team member has a cup in front of them that has an agreed-upon amount (typically, a couple of ounces) of beer or other liquid.

Game Play

Each team has a lead-off player, and these two designated players count to three, clink cups, and drink the contents of their cups. When a player finishes the beer, he or she then places the cup on the edge of the table in front of the player and then tries to use one hand to flip it so that it lands upside down on the table. If the cup does not land properly, the player must place the cup on the edge of the table and try flipping it again. After the cup is flipped properly, only then can the next player on the team take his or her turn, and so forth until one side finishes and wins the round. Games are usually played until one team wins 5 or 10 rounds.

There are some slight variations as to the order in subsequent rounds. Sometimes, the lead-off spot moves to the next two players. In other versions, the losing side must rotate so that its second member moves up to the lead-off position and the former lead-off person moves to the end, while the winning team's lead-off member stays the same.

Beer Pong

Beer pong is another drinking game transported from colleges and parties to concert tailgating. In its most common incarnation, beer pong refers to a game in which one to two people per side attempt to land ping-pong balls into a series of cups containing beer or other liquid across a table. Technically, the name "Beer Pong" refers to this game's forerunner, which involved hitting balls into the cups using ping-pong paddles, but it now commonly refers to the game in which people try to throw the ball into the cups. Let's face it: it's tough enough to direct the balls in the cup with your hand, and it's even more so with a ping-pong paddle.

What You Need to Play

- Plastic cups
- A table, preferably 6 feet or longer
- Beer or other beverage for the cups

Game Setup

There are multiple variations of the game, but there are usually six or ten plastic cups, arranged in a triangle on each side. Beer or other liquid is then poured into each cup. (Typically, about 2–4 ounces per cup are used.) Of course, if you're using hard liquor, the serving size should be adjusted downwards (unless you want to get inebriated quicker).

Game Play

The object of the game is to sink a ball in each of the opposite team's cups. One team takes its turn shooting 1 or 2 ping-pong balls to try to land in the cups.

The Jimmy Buffett Concert Handbook

Each time a ball lands in the cup, someone from the opposing team must drink its contents. In theory, of course, the team forced to drink more will have its performance suffer. The emptied cup is then removed from play, and most games involve "reracking" the cups into a triangle or a diamond when there are 6, 4, and 3 cups left. When there are 2 cups left, the cups are often placed adjacent to each other in a vertical line. When there is just one cup left, the last cup is often centered against the back edge of the table. A turn is over after each person on the team has thrown a ball (or sometimes two balls), and the other side then takes its turn.

A team wins when it sinks balls into all the cups, although the other side is often given a shot to "tie" it if it can clear its remaining cups with the remaining throws it has left. Tiebreakers involve a shortened rematch using a smaller number of cups, often 3 cups.

CHAPTER 4

Living the Parrothead Lifestyle 24/7

Gypsies in the Palace:
Bringing Buffett Home

Once you've experienced the pure joy that is the Buffett tailgate, you may decide that you want to revisit Margaritaville more than once a year. In fact, you can remind yourself of the fun you had with the Phlock by incorporating some of these ideas into your household. Before you know it, you'll be retiring to Key West and vacationing in Jamaica.

- Always keep a batch of Make-Ahead Frozen Margaritas in your freezer. They make any day just a little bit brighter, and unopened containers of them will keep in the freezer for months. There's nothing better than scraping a little frozen margarita into your glass and relaxing on the porch (or in your easy chair) as you contemplate absolutely nothing.

- Buy a hand-decorated Adirondack chair from Margaritaville and sit in it with your favorite drinks. With many themes to choose from, these brightly colored chairs are sure to bring a little cheer to your life. Even the chair's arms are painted with unique little touches, such as a Lost Shaker of Salt or a recipe for margaritas.

○ Get a salt-water aquarium tank and adopt a shark from the pet store. I mean really, can you think of a cooler pet? The companion-ship alone is sure to reduce your stress. And an aquarium shark has the added benefit of reminding you of Jimmy's classic song, "Fins."

○ Celebrate "Talk Like a Pirate Day" on September 19. Spend the day working phrases like, "Arrgh," "Scallywag," and "Shiver Me Timbers" into your everyday conversations, and see how much joy it brings you. It's the one day other than a Buffett concert day when you can act like a pirate and get away with it!

○ Decorate your house with tropical plants. If you can't visit the tropics, you can bring them into your house with some carefully chosen foliage. Pick different types of palms, some bamboo, or perhaps even some cactuses. Or, if you want something a little less classy, buy an inflatable palm tree and stick it in your living room to give it that campy Margaritaville flavor.

- Buy a tropical bird—perhaps even a parrot. The bird's colorful plumage will brighten up your days, and you'll have a unique friend to bring with you to future Buffett tailgates. Birds make great pets, and are much lower maintenance than cats and dogs.

- Listen to Jimmy Buffett's concerts on Radio Margaritaville, either on Sirius Satellite Radio, or online at www.radiomargaritaville.com. It's the perfect soundtrack for your laid-back Parrothead life.

It's Five O'Clock Somewhere: Parrotheads at Work

Working in a cubicle or office can really be a drag, which is probably why several of Jimmy's songs involve working stiffs getting fed up and leaving the job to go on a Caribbean vacation or a drinking binge. Even if you can't leave your office that easily, you can escape the stress by bringing a little of the Margaritaville state of mind into your workspace.

- Customize your computer background with a photo of an exotic locale or a candid shot of you and fellow Parrotheads at last year's tailgate. (We do, however, recommend that you use judgment when choosing a photo, since Big Brother may be watching.)

- Download Buffett-themed desktop icons such as parrots, pirate flags, shark fins, and palm trees to make even the most frustrating work project seem appealing.

- Have a mouse pad made from your favorite Buffett photo, or buy one that features a beach theme. Many online photo companies like Shutterfly make it easy to create personalized accessories like this for your office.

- Keep a dashboard hula girl (or guy) on your desk and make her dance for an instant mood boost.

- Hang a flower lei from your corkboard. Put it on when you're really stressed out, and then close your eyes and pretend you're tailgating. The feeling of the lei on the back of your neck will help you remember those happy days.

- String Buffett-themed mini lights such as margaritas or palm trees in your workspace and turn the dreary fluorescent lights off.

- Put large photos or posters of island sunsets on your walls. If your office doesn't have a window, make a fake one by nailing thick wood molding pieces around the outside edges of your poster and horizontally across the center. Add thinner molding pieces in criss-cross patterns on the centers of the "panes" to make the windows look more authentic.

- Play a nature sounds machine or CD that features seagulls and lapping waves and feel the stress wash away.

- Light a coconut-scented candle or plug in a tropical-scented air freshener. The sweet smell will instantly transport your mind to the beach and mask that stuffy office building smell.

- Draw a pencil-thin moustache on a photo of your boss or evil co-worker. Give them a coconut bra and grass skirt for good measure.

- Keep a blender in the office kitchen. Use it to make virgin (or, in cases of emergency, not-so-virgin) daiquiris but call them "smoothies" so your boss doesn't get suspicious.

- Plug a mini fridge under your desk and stock it with beer. When you just can't take it anymore, get a head start on happy hour while rationalizing that "It's five o'clock somewhere."

The Jimmy Buffett Concert Handbook

Hosting a Buffett Beach Bash

Recapture the joy of those afternoons spent communing with other Parrotheads in the parking lot by having a Jimmy Buffett Beach Bash. Whether you choose to warm up the winter with a temporary tropical paradise or celebrate the dog days of summer instead, you're sure to get a great response. There are endless possibilities for invitation themes inspired by Jimmy's tunes—a beach ball, parrot, shark fin, lobster, beach umbrella, lifeguard chair, pair of flip-flops, pirate ship, or palm tree are all good options. Pick your favorite song and then search online for fun cards featuring your image or make your own with colored paper. Include a suggestion that guests come in tropical or beach attire. Once you've mailed the invites, get a head start on the decorations and food with these ideas.

Décor

- If you don't have real tropical plants (or even if you do), put a few inflatable or light-up palm trees around your living room or in the backyard.

- Light Polynesian torches in the backyard to provide visibility and set the tropical mood.

- String a flower lei garland around the room and have plenty of leis on hand to give guests as they enter. You could also give each female guest a flower to put behind her ear.

- Use baskets of seashells, sand dollars, and starfish to give tables a beachy feel.

- Stick votive candles in bowls and pour sand around them for a pretty table decoration.

- Buy colorful flip-flops at the craft store or discount shoe store and use them to anchor helium-filled balloons in fun shapes.

- Hang a stuffed or tissue-paper parrot or two from a plant hook or light fixture.

Beverages

- Borrow extra blenders from friends and set up a tiki bar area for preparing frozen drinks like piña coladas and daiquiris. Consider hiring a professional bartender or having friends volunteer so the drinks are made fast and with as little mess as possible.

- Freeze a batch of make-ahead strawberry daiquiris for instant gratification.

- Put pretty drink umbrellas, colorful straws, and cocktail swords speared with fruit in your frozen concoctions so guests feel like they're at a beach bar.

- Make colored sugar for use on the rim of strawberry daiquiris. Simply pour sugar into a zip-top plastic bag. Add a few drops of red food coloring and close the bag. Shake to mix. Add more food coloring, a few drops at a time, until the sugar is the desired color. Pour into a saucer and roll the moistened lip of a glass around in it.

Food

- Our Jamaican Jerk Chicken recipe works great as a tropical hors d'oeuvre if you use precut chicken breast tenders instead of chicken breast cutlets. After marinating, skewer each tender before grilling. Serve the chicken on the skewers.

- Slices of homemade Hawaiian-style pizza will disappear in a flash. Use prebaked pizza rounds, such as Boboli, to save time. Top with tomato sauce, basil, shredded mozzarella cheese, grated Parmesan cheese, ham, and pineapple. Bake according to the package directions, and then slice into small wedges or squares with a pizza cutter.

- Set up a station for burgers and dogs featuring toppings such as lettuce, sliced tomatoes, pickles, sliced onions and/or sautéed onions, grilled pineapple slices, bacon, sauerkraut, ketchup, mustard, mayonnaise, A1 sauce, and barbecue sauce.

Music

- Jimmy's already done the work for you when it comes to beach music. Start with the Beaches disc from his box set, "Boats, Beaches, Bars, and Ballads," and then move on to the rest of the set.

- If you prefer more control over your musical fate, make your own playlist of favorite Jimmy Buffett songs, with a few songs from Don Ho, Israel Kamakawiwo'ole, Jack Johnson, and The Beach Boys mixed in.

Planning a Margaritaville Party

When you need a break from the real world, revisit the Margaritaville state of mind by hosting a margarita fiesta. Start with homemade invitations shaped like a margarita glass, look online for printed invites, or use one of Evite's many margarita-themed backgrounds. Consider planning your party as a Cinco de Mayo celebration, or schedule it just after Labor Day as an extension of summer. Once you have the date, it's time to plan the details.

Décor

- Hang strings of chili pepper, cactus, or margarita mini lights around the room.
- Buy or borrow a large sombrero to use as a centerpiece for the food table. You can even fill the brim of the hat with tortilla chips as a serving piece.
- Visit your local plant nursery to purchase a selection of small cacti to help set the mood.

Beverages

- Prepare a freezer-full of make-ahead frozen margaritas—and make some of them strawberry! Be sure to provide plenty of plastic spoons for your guests.

- Have Mexican beers like Corona and Dos Equis on hand for those who can't handle the frozen concoctions.

- Cut limes from end to end to make long, thin wedges for beer bottles. For margarita rims, cut the lime in half around the middle, then place each end open-side-down on the cutting board and cut into six or eight small wedges.

- If you don't have a rim salting plate, simply pour kosher salt on a saucer.

Food

- Serve guacamole and salsa in hand-blown margarita glasses with a bowl of high-quality tortilla chips just in front of them for a nice presentation.

- Cook beef in a slow cooker and shred for make-your-own tacos. Serve with soft tortillas and a selection of toppings, including shredded Monterey Jack cheese, sour cream, lettuce, chopped tomatoes, and green olives.

- Baked chicken quesadillas are a quick and easy crowd-pleaser. Simply spray tortillas with cooking spray and place them on a baking sheet. Top with cheese, precooked fajita-style chicken pieces, and your favorite fillings, and cover with another sprayed tortilla. Bake for about five minutes per side, and then cut into small wedges with a pizza cutter.

Music

Create a playlist that evolves with your night—start with Latin-tinged rhythms like the Buena Vista Social Club and the Gipsy Kings, then segue into a mix of Jimmy Buffett and our Margaritaville Playlist as the margaritas keep flowing.

Margaritaville Playlist

When you're wastin' away again in Margaritaville, there's nothing better than listening to more songs about that tasty concoction and the craziness it brings.

- "It's Five O'Clock Somewhere" (Alan Jackson & Jimmy Buffett, *Alan Jackson: Greatest Hits, Vol. 2*)
- "Raised on Margaritas" (Los Pacaminos, *Los Pacaminos*)
- "1 Tequila, 2 Tequila, 3 Tequila, Floor" (Tim Aaron, *Cut to the Chase*)
- "20 Margaritas" (Big & Rich, *Comin' to Your City*)
- "Senorita Margarita" (Tim McGraw, *A Place in the Sun*)
- "Ten Rounds with Jose Cuervo" (Tracy Byrd, *The Truth About Men*)
- "I Need a Margarita" (Clay Walker, *Rumor Has It*)

- "Cuka Rocka (Extended)" (Chingon, *Mexican Spaghetti Western*)
- "Three Margaritas" (NOMaD: North of Mason-Dixon, *Born and Raised*)
- "Loco (Muy Caliente Mix)" (David Lee Murphy, *The "Loco" Tapes*)

What is a Parrothead Club?

Parrothead clubs are a phenomenon that has come into popularity amongst the Phlock since the 1990s. The original Parrothead club was founded in Atlanta in 1989 by Scott Nickerson. Nickerson's idea was that because he enjoyed meeting people during tailgating at concerts, he should try to get together with those same people more than once a year. The original club was intended to be more than just a fan club, as it would take part in various activities. As of 2007, there are about two hundred such clubs throughout the country. Members of these clubs are, of course, huge fans of Jimmy Buffett and the Buffett lifestyle.

What Do They Do?

Part of the reason for joining these clubs is the camaraderie of other like-minded folks. Another reason is the numerous community and charitable activities in which Parrothead clubs participate. The international umbrella organization of Parrothead clubs estimates that in 2006, clubs donated over $2.6 million and 173,000 volunteer hours to local and national charities. Some clubs create incentives of providing access to Buffett club box tickets for those who participate in a certain number of charity events. And on the social side, Parrothead clubs also typically have monthly happy hours and other social events.

Every year, the Meeting of the Minds, which is the annual gathering of Parrothead clubs and its members, takes place in Key West. In 2006, more than 3,500 Parrotheads attended the celebration.

How to Find Your Local Club

Parrot Heads in Paradise, Inc. is the international organization of Parrothead clubs. Its Web site (www.phip.com) has the comprehensive listing of active Parrothead clubs, their Web sites and contacts. The cost of joining a Parrothead club is not prohibitive—usually only about $20.

How to Start Your Own Parrothead Club

If your hometown doesn't have an active Parrothead club, you can start one. Parrot Heads in Paradise provides the policies (www.phip.com/Policies.asp) and guidelines (www.phip.com/Guidelines.asp) for starting a new club. The main requirements are that a new club cannot be within twenty-five miles of an existing club and must be of open membership. Potential new chapters are encouraged to make sure there is a core group of members, a set meeting spot, and proper organization.

CHAPTER 5

Virtual Margaritaville

Jimmy on the Web

Jimmy Buffett has a huge presence on the Internet, thanks to his extensive web of official sites and the devotion of his Parrothead fans. Here are a few of the best online resources:

www.margaritaville.com
Jimmy Buffett's official Web site.

www.radiomargaritaville.com
Find out when Jimmy Buffett concerts will be played on Radio Margaritaville, or listen to the station online.

www.myspace.com/jimmybuffett
Become one of Jimmy's more than 120,000 MySpace friends and see upcoming concert dates.

www.buffettworld.com
A great unofficial but informative source for Jimmy Buffett information.

www.buffettnews.com

This Web site focuses primarily on information about the tours.

www.orientaltrading.com

A party supply catalog with everything from parrot hats and leis to portable tiki bars.

www.phip.com

Parrotheads in Paradise Inc. is the international organization of Parrothead clubs.

About the Authors

Elizabeth Encarnacion is a Seasoned Vet of Jimmy Buffett tailgates whose parents taught her to always have a batch of frozen margaritas in the freezer in case of emergency. She is a freelance editor and author whose works include the upcoming *Girls' Guide to Campfire Activities* from Applesauce Press, a novelization of the classic TV special *Rudolph the Red-Nosed Reindeer*, and the four-book *Buildings at Work* series. She also cofounded FlirtyGirl Productions, a book packager that specializes in cutting-edge teen entertainment. Visit her on the Web at www.elizabethencarnacion.com.

John Encarnacion experienced his first Jimmy Buffett show in 1996, and has been a regular at tailgates and concerts every year since 1999. When he's not wastin' away again in Margaritaville, he works as an attorney in Philadelphia. Until now, most of John's writing credits have been boring legal articles.

Photo and Illustration Credits

Page 3: ©iStockphoto.com/Kitch Bain, ©iStockphoto.com/Joe Cicak; page 6: ©iStockphoto.com/Rebecca Ellis, Courtesy of Julie Simmons; page 7: Courtesy of John Encarnacion, Courtesy of Julie Simmons, Courtesy of Elaina "Lainy" Mastromarc; page 8:©iStockphoto.com/Stephanie Phillips; page 8: ©iStockphoto.com/Radovan Kraker, ©iStockphoto.com/Andrey Stenkin; page 10: ©iStockphoto.com/DaddyBit; page 11: ©iStockphoto.com/Kristoffer Hamilton; page 12: ©iStockphoto.com/Donna Franklin; page 13: Courtesy of Elaina "Lainy" Mastromarc; page 14: Courtesy of John Encarnacion; page 15: ©iStockphoto.com/Madeleine Openshaw; page 16: ©iStockphoto.com/Robert Kohlhuber; page 17: ©iStockphoto.com/Mark Goddard; page 18: ©iStockphoto.com/Julie Masson; page 20: ©iStockphoto.com/Plainview; page 28: ©iStockphoto.com/Jeremy Edwards; page 30: ©iStockphoto.com/Greg Nicholas; page 31: ©iStockphoto.com/Béatrice Pautaire; page 33: Courtesy of Julie Simmons; page 34: ©iStockphoto.com/Lily Rosen-Zohar; page 36: Courtesy of John Encarnacion; page 37: Courtesy of Elaina "Lainy" Mastromarc; page 39: ©iStockphoto.com/Paul Johnson; page 40: ©iStockphoto.com/Skip ODonnell; page 42: ©iStockphoto.com/Christopher O Driscoll; page 43: ©iStockphoto.com/Jason Lugo; page 45: ©iStockphoto.com/Paul Johnson; page 46: ©iStockphoto.com/Matthew Cole; page 47: ©iStockphoto.com/Lexx; page 48: Courtesy of John Encarnacion; page 49: ©iStockphoto.com/Christine Balderas; page 50: Courtesy of Elaina "Lainy" Mastromarc; page 51: ©iStockphoto.com/Dóri O'Connell; page 52: ©iStockphoto.com/Alex Nikada; page 55: ©iStockphoto.com/Rick Hoffart; page 59: ©iStockphoto.com/Sawayasu Tsuji; page 60: ©iStockphoto.com/Pascal Genest; page 62: ©iStockphoto.com/Lee Feldstein; page 63: Courtesy of John Encarnacion; page 64: Courtesy of Elaina "Lainy" Mastromarc; page 66–67: Courtesy of Elaina "Lainy" Mastromarc; page 68: ©iStockphoto.com/Eric Isselée; page 70: Courtesy of Elaina "Lainy" Mastromarc; page 72: ©iStockphoto.com/Justin Horrocks; page 73–74: Courtesy of Elaina "Lainy" Mastromarc; page 76: Courtesy of Elaina "Lainy" Mastromarc; page 77: Courtesy of John Encarnacion; page 78: ©iStockphoto.com/Roman Chmiel; page 79: ©iStockphoto.com/Christine Balderas; page 81: ©iStockphoto.com/Fresh

Vectors; page 82: ©iStockphoto.com/Jon Patton; page 83: ©iStockphoto.com/ Steve Dibblee; page 85: ©iStockphoto.com/Tomasz Tulik; page 86: ©iStockphoto. com/Spauln; page 88: ©iStockphoto.com/Matt Knannlein; page 91: Courtesy of Elaina "Lainy" Mastromarc; page 92: ©iStockphoto.com/Yong Hian Lim; page 95: ©iStockphoto.com/The New Dawn Singers Inc.; page 96: ©iStockphoto. com/Kelly Cline; page 97: ©iStockphoto.com/kativ; page 98: ©iStockphoto.com/ ccaetano; page 100: ©iStockphoto.com/Greg Nicholas; page 102: ©iStockphoto. com/Charles Cihon; 104: ©iStockphoto.com/Mach New Media; page 105: ©iStockphoto.com/Olga Lyubkina; page 106: ©iStockphoto.com/Lisa F. Young; page 107: ©iStockphoto.com/Skip ODonnell; page 109: ©iStockphoto.com/ Danny Hooks; page 110: ©iStockphoto.com/firina; page 112: ©iStockphoto.com/ Feng Yu; page 113: ©iStockphoto.com/Philip Pellat; page 113: ©iStockphoto.com/ Christine Balderas; page 115: ©iStockphoto.com/Daniele Barioglio; page 116: ©iStockphoto.com/Plainview; page 118: ©iStockphoto.com/Enrico Fianchini; page 119: ©iStockphoto.com/Michael Valdezi; page 120: ©iStockphoto.com/ endrille; page 122: ©iStockphoto.com/Christine Balderas; page 124: Courtesy of Elaina "Lainy" Mastromarc; page 126: ©iStockphoto.com/Johanna Goodyear; page 127: ©iStockphoto.com/A-Digit; page 128: Courtesy of Elaina "Lainy" Mastromarc; page 131: ©iStockphoto.com/Elnur Amikishiyev; page 132: Courtesy of Elaina "Lainy" Mastromarc; page 134: ©iStockphoto.com/William Berry; page 135: ©iStockphoto.com/konradlew, ©iStockphoto.com/Skip ODonnel; page 136: ©iStockphoto.com/Roberto A Sanchez; page 137: ©iStockphoto.com/Steve Dibblee; page 139: ©iStockphoto.com/Digital Food Shots; page 140: Courtesy of Elaina "Lainy" Mastromarc; page 141: ©iStockphoto.com/Christophe Testi; page 142: ©iStockphoto.com/Michal Rozanski; page 143: ©iStockphoto.com/Ivan Mateev; page 144: ©iStockphoto.com/Liv Friis-Larsen; page 145: ©iStockphoto.com/Tim Starkey; page 146: ©iStockphoto.com/Chiya Li; paage 147: ©iStockphoto.com/ Yong Hian Lim; page 148: ©iStockphoto.com/Floortje; page 151: ©iStockphoto. com/Linda Bucklin; page 153: ©iStockphoto.com/Brendon De Suza; page 154: ©iStockphoto.com/CostinT; page 155: ©iStockphoto.com/Michal Rozanski

About Cider Mill Press Book Publishers

Good ideas ripen with time. From seed to harvest, Cider Mill Press strives to bring fine reading, information, and entertainment together between the covers of its creatively crafted books. Our Cider Mill bears fruit twice a year, publishing a new crop of titles each spring and fall.

Visit us on the Web at
www.cidermillpress.com
or write to us at
12 Port Farm Road
Kennebunkport, Maine 04046

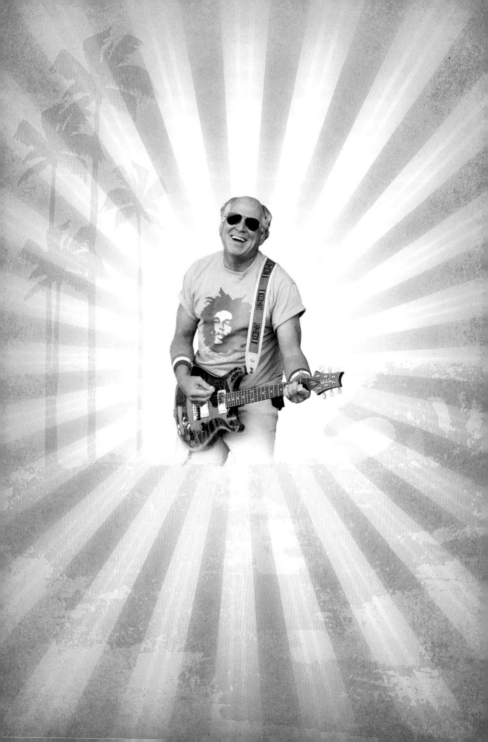